International Directory of Psychology

A Guide to People,
Places, and Policies

International Directory of Psychology

A Guide to People,
Places, and Policies

Benjamin B. Wolman

Plenum Press · New York and London

Library of Congress Cataloging in Publication Data

Wolman, Benjamin B
International directory of psychology.

Includes index.
1. Psychology — Societies, etc. — Directories. 2. Psychology — Study
and teaching — Directories. 3. Psychological research — Directories.
4. Psychologists — Directories. 5. Psychological literature. I. Title.
[DNLM: 1. Psychology. BF38 W865p]
BF30.W64   150   78-27868
ISBN 0-306-40209-2

©1979 Plenum Press, New York
A Division of Plenum Publishing Corporation
227 West 17th Street, New York, N.Y. 10011

Printed in the United States of America

Foreword

In the past several decades, psychology has grown so rapidly in many countries that no one has been able to keep up-to-date on more than a handful of countries. To be sure, the highly developed countries of North America, Western Europe, Japan, and Australia have generally had well-known national psychological societies for most of this century, and considerable information about their universities and institutes has been published at one time or another. But even in these more highly developed countries, the rapid changes of recent years are not well known. In any event, what information has been published is scattered so widely that it is hardly accessible when needed.

Still less well known is the growth of psychology in the developing countries of Latin America, Asia, and Africa, and at least for Western readers, even the modern nations of Eastern Europe and the Soviet Union are relatively unknown. Only recently have most Western psychologists become aware of the fact that psychology as they know it is provincial. With more than half of the world's highly trained psychologists in Canada and the United States, which together devote far more of their national resources to psychological research than is true of any other countries in the world, it is not surprising that the North American journals, psychological associations, institutes, clinics, and other manifestations of psychology have completely dominated the field, at least until recently. The increasing amount of travel, exchange of ideas, and participation in international meetings by psychologists throughout the world, have helped to break down this provincialism that is especially characteristic of many psychologists in North America.

With the growth of psychology since World War II, international organizations have sponsored congresses and international projects that have brought together many thousands of psychologists. The International Union of Psychological Science was formally established in 1951 at the XIIIth International Congress of Psychology held in Stockholm, Sweden. The International Union is the only international organization which has as its members national psychological societies rather than individual psychologists. Today the Union has 42 national societies from all parts of the world. A mere 25 years ago, the 11 charter members of the Union were all national societies of psychology from Europe and North America, with the exception of Japan. This striking change has been accompanied by regional international associations, as well. The largest of these, the Interamerican Society of Psychology, has held 16 congresses throughout the Americas and is now the primary mode of professional and scientific exchange for thousands of psychologists in the countries of South and Central America. Congresses held by the International Association of Applied Psychology, the International Association for Cross-Cultural Psychology, the International Council of Psychology, and a score of other smaller specialized groups have likewise contributed greatly to a better understanding of the different patterns of development in psychology throughout the world.

For those psychologists fortunate enough to travel widely and to exchange ideas with colleagues in other countries, a firsthand acquaintance with foreign institutions and the development of a network of corresponding psychologists can give one deeper insight into both the strengths and limitations of psychology within his own country. But what about the overwhelming majority of psychologists throughout the world who are not so fortunate? Deeply concerned about these issues and how best to provide authoritative and objective information about psychology throughout the world, Benjamin Wol-

man embarked upon a systematic survey that took several
years to complete. The results of this work are presented in this
book. In most cases the information has been provided by
well-known international leaders who are fully acquainted with
the development of psychology in their own countries. An added bonus at the end of each country is a concluding note on
opportunities for foreign psychologists.

A compendium summarizing the highlights of psychology,
country by country, provides for the first time in one place a
convenient reference for all of us who have any interest in
psychology outside of our own familiar national and regional
associations. The reader should not be surprised if some information is out-of-date, since the rapidity of change in many
countries is so great that it is impossible to be fully accurate and
up-to-date, no matter how hard one tries. It is to be hoped that
this first edition of *International Directory of Psychology* will
create sufficient interest and response that a revised edition
can be published in the near future.

WAYNE H. HOLTZMAN
Secretary-General
International Union of Psychological Science

Preface

Several years ago, Bertrand Russell described as the following the role psychology plays in modern life:

> In regard to human knowledge there are two questions that may be asked: first, what do we know? and second, how do we know it? The first of these questions is answered by science, which tries to be as impersonal and as dehumanized as possible. In the resulting survey of the universe it is natural to start with astronomy and physics, which deal with what is large and what is universal; life and mind, which are rare and have, apparently, little influence on the course of events, must occupy a minor position in this impartial survey. But in relation to our second question—namely, how do we come by our knowledge—psychology is the most important of the sciences. Not only is it necessary to study psychologically the processes by which we draw inferences, but it turns out that all the data upon which our inferences should be based are psychological in character; that is to say, they are experiences of single individuals. The apparent publicity of our world is part delusive and in part inferential; all the raw material of our knowledge consists of mental events in the lives of separate people. In this region, therefore, psychology is supreme. (*Human Knowledge: Its Scope and Limits*)

The future historians of civilization will probably call our century the century of psychology. Psychology today has entered several fields of human endeavor. It dominates human relations in the economic processes—engineering, industry, aviation, marketing, and advertising—and in politics and warfare. Education, mental health, vocational choice and guidance, and several other fields are staffed, guided, and supervised by hosts of highly skilled psychologists around the world.

In spring of 1973 I was invited to deliver the keynote address at the XIVth Interamerican Congress of Psychology in São Paulo, Brazil. During my stay in Brazil, I had the opportunity of meeting a great many psychologists from Latin America, Canada, the United States, and several European countries. In our informal meetings we discovered how diversified are our interests and activities and how little we know of each other.

The aim of this volume is to facilitate the exchange of information among psychologists around the world. Dependability and precision have been the guideposts of this project. Accordingly, instead of relying on impressionistic descriptions by arbitrarily chosen psychologists, I addressed my inquiries to the executive offices of the national psychological organizations, to governmental bodies, and to other authorized persons.

From the inception of this project it has been clear that one cannot expect uniformity in the information supplied by national psychological organizations, by governmental agencies, and, in some cases, by competent individuals. The sheer quantitative differences between 50,000 psychologists in the United States and a handful in some other countries affects the nature of the profession and its status. Also, ideological differences and divergent viewpoints reflect the way psychologists view themselves.

Accordingly, three versions of a questionnaire were prepared: The detailed main Questionnaire A was geared to the well-established national organizations; the shorter Questionnaire B was prepared for countries that could not supply the detailed information requested in Questionnaire A; and finally, Questionnaire C was applied whenever the respondents asked for a brief set of questions. All three questionnaires are included in this volume.

The respondents requested a certain degree of freedom in organizing their information and, after receiving all the replies, I have appended, whenever necessary, additional information, using a variety of printed sources and correspondence with competent individuals in various countries.

I am taking this opportunity to thank all the individuals and organizations who contributed to this volume, especially Wayne Holtzman, the secretary-general of the International Union of Psychological Science (IUPS); Gerardo Marín, secretary-general of the Inter-American Society of Psychology; and the staff members of the American Psychological Association.

BENJAMIN B. WOLMAN

Contributors

C. J. Adcock, *New Zealand*
Reynaldo Alarcón, *Peru*
Arrigo Leonardo Angelini, *Brazil*
Rubén Ardilla, *Colombia*
Nezahat Arkun, *Turkey*
Ahmed M. Azzam, *Egypt*
Erik Becker, *Venezuela*
J. Bierzwińska, *Poland*
C. Alan Boneau, *United States*
P. J. Carnibella, *Bolivia*
Jae-ho Cha, *Korea*
Rodolfo Panay Claros, *Ecuador*
Singgih D. Cunersa, *Indonesia*
John L. M. Binnie Dawson, *Hong Kong*
R. Díaz-Guerrero, *Mexico*
Remy Droz, *Switzerland*
G. d'Ydewalle, *Belgium*
Mordechai Eran, *Israel*
Carlos Luis La Fuenta Glecha, *Paraguay*
R. D. Griesel, *South Africa*
E. Hashemi, *Iran*
Ralph R. Hetherington, *United Kingdom*
Wayne H. Holtzman, *United States*

Lambros Houssiadas, *Greece*
Shinkuro Iwahara, *Japan*
Mohamed Kazem, *Qatar*
Julietta Lagomarsino, *Uruguay*
Boris F. Lomov, *Union of Soviet Socialist Republics*
José Mallart, *Spain*
Gerardo Marín, *Colombia*
Vladimir N. Martynenko, *Ukranian Soviet Socialist Republic*
James McLoone, *Ireland*
Luigi Meschieri, *Italy*
H. Minami, *Japan*
Natividad Munarriz, *Philippines*
Charles Roger Myers, *Canada*
F. D. Naylor, *Australia*
Joseph Notterman, *United States*
Joseph Nuttin, *Belgium*
Robert Pages, *France*
S. M. Poghni, *Pakistan*
Harley O. Preston, *United States*
Edwin Terry Prothro, *Lebanon*
N. Sbhandoa, *Fiji*
Franco Lo Presti Seminério, *Brazil*
T. E. Shanmugam, *India*
Ayan Bahadur Shrestha, *Nepal*
J. V. Spiteri, *Malta*
A. M. Stuyling de Lange, *Netherlands*
Pablo Antonio Thalassinos, *Panama*
Hermán Berwart Torrens, *Chile*
V. P. Vassilopoulos, *Cyprus*
Dogomil Velichkov, *Bulgaria*
Constantin Voicu, *Romania*
Hans Weltzer, *Denmark*

Liana Ortiz Wolf, *Chile*
Raymond H. T. Wong, *Singapore*
E. A. Yoloye, *Nigeria*
R. O. Zucha, *Austria*

Contents

Introductory Letter

I am pleased to inform you that I am beginning the preparation of a reference book in psychology which is intended to serve as a directory of the psychological profession in every country in the world. This volume, to be entitled *International Directory of Psychology,* will describe in detail the organizational structure and functions of the national psychological organizations, the educational and research facilities in each country, the legal status and occupations of psychologists, and the major publications in the field.

You will find enclosed a copy of a questionnaire addressed to the Executive Officer of the National Psychological Organization. I shall greatly appreciate your having the questionnaire answered and returned to me as soon as is possible. Please feel free to make any changes that would make the questionnaire more serviceable and more applicable to your country.

With deep appreciation for your cooperation, I am

Sincerely yours,

Benjamin B. Wolman
Editor-in-Chief
of the International Encyclopedia
of Psychiatry, Psychology,
Psychoanalysis and Neurology

Enclosure

The Questionnaires

Questionnaire A

The information requested in this questionnaire is intended to provide comprehensive information concerning the psychological profession in your country. If the questions do not cover an area of the profession that you feel is important, please include information on this area as an addendum to the questionnaire. If a question is not applicable to your situation, please modify it accordingly. Thank you for your cooperation.

I. National Psychological Organization
   1. Official name of organization
   2. Address of central office
   3. Official language(s) used
   4. Internal structure (describe briefly)
   5. Membership:
      a. Total number of members
      b. Categories of membership (associate, fellow, etc.) and number of members
   6. Names of divisions and/or sections (according to professional group, special interest, etc.)
   7. General admission requirements and special requirements for each membership category and division
   8. Major activities of organization (describe briefly)
II. Education and Training of Psychologists
   1. Educational facilities:

      a. Number of schools or institutes offering training in psychology
      b. Types of degrees or diplomas offered and number of institutions offering each
      c. Average number of students in each degree or diploma program
      d. Governmental supervisory system for accreditation
      e. Influence of the national psychological organization on the educational system

III. Legal Status
    1. Licensing and certification requirements and procedures (degrees, examinations, etc.)
    2. Professional ethical code and disciplinary procedures

IV. Research and Publications
    1. Research facilities (describe the type of work being done, resources available, and grants or other remuneration obtainable):
      a. Government agencies
      b. Research facilities associated with universities
      c. Private research centers
    2. Journals (please give name, address, and frequency of publication):
      a. Journal(s) published by national psychological organization
      b. Other professional journals
    3. Books (estimate number published per year in each category):
      a. Scholarly books for the profession
      b. Reference books (directories, dictionaries, handbooks)
      c. Educational textbooks

V. Occupational Distribution
For each of the types of jobs in psychology listed below, please estimate the number of psychologists working in the particular field. If there are types of

positions that psychologists hold in your country that are not included in this list, please add them.

Type of Job

1. University professors
2. Teachers in secondary education
3. School psychologists and guidance counselors
4. Vocational counselors
5. Rehabilitation counselors
6. Clinical psychologists in hospitals
7. Clinical psychologists in private practice
8. Research workers and administrators
9. Industrial psychologists
10. Other

VI. Opportunities for Foreign Psychologists

Questionnaire B

The information requested in this questionnaire aims at providing comprehensive information concerning the psychological profession in your country. Please feel free to omit questions which are not appropriate for your country. You may describe issues not covered in the questionnaire and change the order of the questions.

Thank you for your cooperation.

I. Introduction
II. Education and Training in Psychology
III. Occupations of Psychologists
IV. Legal Status and Governmental Supervision
V. Research
VI. Publications
   1. Journals
   2. Books
VII. National Organization of Psychologists
   1. Name and Address
   2. Internal Structure

3. Membership
4. Special Divisions
5. Major Activities
VIII. Opportunities for Foreign Psychologists

Questionnaire C

In response to your request for a simple questionnaire, please find enclosed seven brief questions. Kindly answer them in as detailed a manner as possible.

Thank you for your cooperation.

1. Introduction
2. Organizations of psychologists in your country, their inner structure, membership, divisions, etc.
3. Education and training of psychologists
4. Research and publications
5. Practice of psychology in your country, such as teaching, clinical practice (hospitals, private practice), industrial psychology, etc.
6. The legal status of psychologists in your country
7. Opportunities for foreign psychologists

International Union of Psychological Science (IUPS)[1]

The International Union of Psychological Science (IUPS) was established in July 1951 at the XIIIth International Congress of Psychology in Stockholm, Sweden. The charter members of the IUPS were the 11 national psychological associations from Belgium, France, Germany, Italy, Japan, Netherlands, Norway, Sweden, Switzerland, the United Kingdom, and the United States.

At the present time the following 41 national psychological associations are members of the IUPS:

Argentina Psychological Society
Australian Psychological Society
Belgian Psychological Society
Brazilian Psychological Association
Bulgarian Psychological Society
Canadian Psychological Association
Colombian Federation of Psychology
Psychologists' Union of Cuba
Czechoslovakia Psychological Society
Danish Psychological Association
Finnish Psychological Society
French Psychological Society
Federation of German Psychological Associations

[1]Based on the report of Wayne H. Holtzman, secretary-general of the IUPS, to the XXIst International Congress of Psychology in Paris.

Society for Psychology of the German Democratic
Republic
Hong Kong Psychological Society
Hungarian Psychological Scientific Association
Indian Psychological Association
Psychological Association of Iran
Psychological Society of Ireland
Israel Psychological Association
Italian Society of Scientific Psychology
Japanese Psychological Association
Korean Psychological Association
Mexican Society of Psychology
Netherlands Psychological Association
New Zealand Psychological Society, Inc.
Norwegian Psychological Association
Psychological Association of the Philippines
Polish Psychological Association
Romanian Psychological Association
South African Psychological Association
Spanish Society of Psychology
Swedish Psychological Association
Swiss Society of Psychology
Turkish Psychological Association
USSR: Soviet Psychological Association
UK: British Psychological Society
USA: American Psychological Association
Uruguayan Psychological Society
Association of Venezuelan Psychologists
Yugoslav Psychological Association.

The objectives of the IUPS are:

1. To develop the exchange of ideas and scientific information between psychologists of different countries,
   and in particular to organize international congresses
   and other meetings on subjects of general or special
   interest in psychology.
2. To contribute to psychological documentation in

different countries by fostering international exchange of publications of all kinds, including reviews, films, and biographies.

3. To aid scholars of different countries to go abroad to universities, laboratories, libraries, and other institutions.
4. To foster the exchange of students and of young research workers.
5. To collaborate with other international and national organizations in matters of mutual interest.
6. To engage in such other activities as will further the development of the science of psychology.

Representatives from the 41 member societies constitute the general assembly, which has final authority for union operations and policy. The assembly meets only during the international congresses once every 4 years (formerly every 3 years). Composed of one or two official delegates from each national society, depending upon the size of the society, the assembly elects a president, two vice-presidents, and 10 additional members of the executive committee. The executive committee, in turn, appoints a secretary-general, a deputy secretary-general, and a treasurer, who provide administrative continuity and also serve as members of the executive committee in handling ongoing work of the union in the period between official meetings of the general assembly. The executive committee meets annually.

There is no paid secretariat; all officers, committee chairmen, and delegates contribute their time and services in supporting the aims and objectives of the union.

Since 1966 the IUPS has published the *International Journal of Psychology.* The address of the secretary-general of the IUPS is:

Dr. Wayne H. Holtzman
The Hogg Foundation for Mental Health
University of Texas
Austin, Texas 78712
United States of America

Inter-American Society of Psychology (SIP)[1]

Introduction

The Inter-American Society of Psychology (Sociedad Interamericana de Psicología, SIP) was founded in 1951 with the aim "to promote knowledge, improvement and protection of professional psychology in North, Central and South Americas."

The official name of the organization is Sociedad Interamericana de Psicología—Inter-American Society of Psychology (SIP).

The address of the central office is:

Apartado Aéreo 32501
Bogotá, Colombia
South America

The official languages are Spanish, English, and Portuguese.

Internal Structure

The society has a board of governors composed of the following officers: past president (elected), president (elected), president-elect (elected), vice-president for the United States

---

[1]Based on information supplied by Gerardo Marín, secretary-general.

and Canada (elected), vice-president for Mexico, Central America, and the Caribbean (elected), vice-president for South America (elected), treasurer (elected), secretary-general (appointed), executive secretary for the United States and Canada (appointed), executive secretary for Mexico, Central America, and the Caribbean (appointed), executive secretary for South America (appointed).

The board of governors conducts, manages, and controls the business of the society. The president is the head of the board of governors and the secretary-general is the executive officer. The secretary-general carries on all general businesses of the society, is in charge of the central office, conducts the official correspondence of the society, and maintains all records.

The elected officers are chosen by general vote of the members; the elections are conducted by mail. The appointed officers are chosen by the president and serve for a period of 2 years.

Membership

The society has a total of 1,200 members; there are three kinds of members: regular (over 1,100), honorary (1), and life (26).

Membership Requirements

Members of the society shall hold an academic or professional degree in psychology appropriate to the prevalent norms in the country in which they reside or an equivalent in training or experience. Degrees in fields closely related to psychology are acceptable provided the applicant has demonstrated interest, competence, and experience in the field of psychology. Members shall hold membership in recognized professional or scientific national organizations where such organizations exist. References from two psychologists may be required. Requests for life membership must be initiated by the member immediately upon retirement and/or physical disability. Honorary members are chosen at the discretion of the board of governors.

Major Activities

Meetings. The SIP sponsors the Inter-American Congresses of Psychology that are held every 2 years in different parts of the Americas. The XIV Congress was held in 1973 in São Paulo, Brazil, with an attendance of about 3,500; the XV Congress was held in Bogotá, Colombia, with an approximate attendance of 3,200; the XVI Congress was held in 1978 in Miami, Florida, with the same attendance. Congress participants include a large number of nonmembers as well as students of psychology. An average of 350 to 500 papers are presented during the congresses with a wide participation from almost every country in the Americas.

Other Activities. The society organized a committee on publications, which studied and translated a series of books into Spanish that were considered to be of special relevance. These books were published by Editorial Trillas in Mexico City.

The society has organized group trips for its members to the several Inter-American Congresses of Psychology, the XXI World Congress of Psychology, and the People's Republic of China. The SIP maintains a very active exchange program of scholars and professionals between the different countries in the Americas. The central office coordinates information regarding researchers who wish to volunteer their sabbatical time, vacations, or leaves of absence as well as institutions willing to receive the visit of a particular researcher and/or professional.

Every 2 years the SIP awards the Inter-American Psychology Award to an English-speaking psychologist and a Spanish-speaking psychologist who have contributed to the development of psychology as a science and/or a profession. The first awards were given in 1976 to mark the 25th anniversary of the society.

Publications

Journal. The SIP publishes the *Revista Interamericana de Psicología/Inter-American Journal of Psychology* (quarterly). The *Revista* is distributed free to all SIP members; its first number was published in 1967. The *Revista* publishes scientific research reports, comments, and book reviews in English, Spanish, and Portuguese. The editor is Horacio Rimoldi (CIIPME, Habana 3870, Buenos Aires, Argentina) and the managing editor is Gerardo Marín (Apartado Aéreo 32501, Bogotá, Colombia).

Books. The SIP has sponsored and recommended the publication of a series of books within the Psychology Library of Editorial Trillas of Mexico City. Among them Trillas has published Osgood's *Experimental Psychology;* Holtzman *et al.*'s *Inkblot Perception and Personality;* Young and Veldam's *Introductory Statistics for the Behavioral Sciences;* Mussen *et al.*'s *Child Development and Personality;* Thorndike and Hagen's *Measurement and Evaluation in Psychology and Education.*

The SIP has published nine issues of a members' directory. The 1963 and 1967 directories contained a selected members' bibliography. A new directory is scheduled for 1979 publication.

The SIP has also published the proceedings of most of the Inter-American Congresses of Psychology, which contain the papers presented at the congresses, as well as abstracts.

THE COUNTRIES

African Countries[1]

Introduction

A description of countries that supplied detailed information (Egypt, Nigeria, and South Africa) follows in alphabetical order. A general description of some African countries is given below.

The Arab north African countries are Algeria, Libya, Morocco, Tunisia, and Egypt. (The latter supplied detailed information.) The University of Algiers offers courses in psychology and also a diploma in psychology, most often in the field of child and educational psychology.

The universities in Algiers, Morocco, and Tunisia have been under French influence, and more of their instructors are trained in France. None of these three countries has developed higher training priorities for professional psychologists.

The Libyan University in Bengazi offers courses in educational psychology.

Several black African countries, such as Cameroon, Central African Republic, Chad, Congo, Dabrovney, Gabon, Ivory Coast, Malagasy, and Senegal, have been influenced by the French academic system. The universities in Tananarive (Malagasy), Dakar (Senegal), and others offer psychology within the framework of the humanity division (Faculté des Lettres et Sciences Humaines). The universities of Dakar and Tananarive offer certificates in psychology, and the Dakar University also grants a doctor's degree.

Most of the central and eastern African states, such as

[1]Based on information supplied by various sources.

3

Kenya, Malasi, Rhodesia, Tanzania, Uganda, and Zambia, have been under British influence. The Salisbury University in Rhodesia offers advanced training in psychology. Instruction in psychology, with emphasis on educational psychology, is offered by the University of Liberia and the two colleges in Monrovia, Liberia. The universities in Leopoldville, Elisabethville, and Stanleyville in Zaire (former Belgian Congo) offer advanced study in psychology covering such diversified areas as general, developmental, educational, clinical, comparative, industrial, and social psychology.

Nigeria, Ghana, and Sierra Leone in West Africa have more advanced instruction in psychology. The University of Ghana offers master's degrees in general and educational psychology. The Ibaden University in Nigeria grants Ph.D. degrees.

Research

A great part of African research is conducted by American and European psychologists mostly interested in cross-cultural issues. African psychologists affiliated with medical schools and psychiatry have been involved in etiological and symptomatological studies of mental disorders, especially cultural determinants of psychoses. Several African psychologists have conducted research in developmental, educational, and social psychology as well as in testing and measurements.

In 1963 a research center devoted to social and educational psychology was established at the Dakar University and research in clinical fields was initiated by Fann Hospital at Dakar. A social research center has been developed by the Zambia University. The Lovanium University in Leopoldville conducts research in educational and personnel psychology.

Highly diversified research has been conducted in the various universities. Psychometrics has been one of the most intriguing issues. Psychologists in black Africa compared the aptitudes and achievements of African populations to non-Africans and tried to develop culture-free tests and tests adjusted to the local sociocultural climate. Considerable attention has been given to developmental psychology, perception and cognitive processes, educational psychology, and sociopsychological aspects of personality.

Publications

Many works of African psychologists are published in France, the United Kingdom, and the United States. *Revue de Psycho-Pathologie Africaine* is published by the Fann Hospital Center in Dakar, Senegal.

Occupational Distribution

Most African psychologists teach in teachers' colleges, medical schools, and universities. Some are involved in research and governmental jobs.

Opportunities for Foreign Psychologists

African universities welcome psychologists from European countries, the United States, and Canada to teach on a permanent or visiting professorship basis. Inquiries should be directed to the consulates and diplomatic missions around the world or directly to the particular universities. Their addresses can be obtained from the respective consulates and diplomatic missions.

Argentina[1]

Introduction

The first psychological laboratory in Argentina was organized by Horacio Pinero in 1898 in Buenos Aires. Wundt's disciple, Carl Jesinghaus, settled in Buenos Aires in 1912 and a few years later Enrique Mouchet established the Institute of Psychology at the Buenos Aires University. Between 1935 and 1945 Mouchet published *Anales del Instituto de Psicología de la Universidad de Buenos Aires.*

National Organizations

Most Argentinian psychologists belong to the
Sociedad Argentina de Psicología
Avenida Santa Fé 1145
Buenos Aires, Argentina
The official language is Spanish.
In 1962 another association was formed, namely the
Asociación de Psicólogos
Ugarteche 3050
Buenos Aires, Argentina
Both societies hold scientific conferences and seminars.

Education and Training

There are eight national universities in Argentina. Six of them offer intensive programs in psychology. They are the

---

[1]Based on information supplied by various sources.

universities of Buenos Aires, Córdoba, Cuyo, La Plata, Litural, and Tucumán.

At the National University of Buenos Aires the Department of Psychology is a part of the Faculty of Philosophy and Letters. The department offers training in experimental, social, clinical, and developmental psychology. The Buenos Aires University grants the licentiate and doctoral degrees and has a special department of developmental psychology and psychopathology and a research center of psychological studies.

Other universities in Argentina, public and private, follow a similar program of study leading to licentiate and Ph.D. degrees. Some universities offer special training in industrial, educational, and physiological psychology. The clinical area is strongly represented in Argentina's universities.

The Buenos Aires University conducts research in clinical and developmental fields. The Cuyo University is mostly concerned with educational psychology, the Tucumán with psychometrics, and La Plata with perception and psychophysiology.

Publications

The Argentinian National Psychological Society, the Sociedad, publishes the *Revista Argentina de Psicología.*

The National University of Buenos Aires publishes the *Bulletin of the Departments of Psychology and Psychopathology.*

The National University of Cuyo publishes the *Annals of the Institute of Psychoeducational Research.*

Occupational Distribution

Psychologists in Argentina work in several fields, in addition to university teaching and research. Many of them work in hospitals, clinics, and child guidance and social welfare centers, and some are involved in private psychotherapeutic practice. School and industrial psychology are the other areas of work for psychologists in Argentina.

The Center of Interdisciplinary Research in Mathematical and Experimental Psychology in Buenos Aires engages in research in mathematical psychology.

Opportunities for Foreign Psychologists

Foreign experts, especially in industrial and social psychology, are welcome on a permanent or prolonged visitor's basis. Most universities offer 1-year or longer visiting professorships to foreign experts. The command of Spanish is essential.

Inquiries should be directed to particular universities and governmental agencies.

Australia[1]

Introduction

In 1850 there was but one psychologist in Australia, Barzillai
Quaife, who taught psychology in the College of Sydney (today, Sydney University). Since 1883 psychology, especially
child psychology, was taught in the so-called normal schools
and other teacher training institutions. Starting in 1900 most
teacher training was conducted in teachers' colleges, some of
which offered a diversified program in various psychological
fields, especially educational psychology.

Psychology was taught in the Australian universities in
philosophy departments under the heading of "moral" or
"mental" philosophy. From about 1914 separate psychology
departments were established, and from as late as 1955 all
Australian universities have had psychology departments independent from philosophy. In 1920, the first government-oper-
ated psychological clinic was established by the state of Tas-
mania, and in the late 1920s several industrial psychology
centers were put in operation. The Australian Psychological
Society was formed in 1944.

National Organization

Almost all Australian psychologists are members of the
Australian Psychological Society (APS), which has about

[1]Based on information supplied by F. D. Naylor, general secretary of the Australian Psychological Society, and other sources.

9

2,600 members. Prior to the formation of the APS, most Australian psychologists were members of the Australian branch of the British Psychological Society. In 1966 the Australian Psychological Society became independent from the British society.
The address of the APS is:
                    Australian Psychological Society
                    National Science Center
                    191 Royal Parade
                    Parkville, Victoria 3052
                    Australia
The official language is English.

Internal Structure

The governing body of the APS is the elected council. The council appoints various committees. The APS holds an annual conference in August, and during the conference an annual general meeting of the society is held.

Membership

The membership of the APS is composed of honorary fellows, fellows, members, associate members, affiliates, student subscribers, and foreign affiliates. The two major classes of members in the APS are (1) members and (2) associate members. To be admitted to full membership one must have obtained a proper degree based on postgraduate courses of supervised training and/or research extending over a period of not less than 2 years full time, or an equivalent period of time of supervised experience.

A person who shall satisfy the council that he holds such other qualifications as the council may accept and who is elected as hereinafter provided may also become a member. To become an associate member a person shall have successfully completed a sequence of 4 years of academic training approved for the purpose of associate membership of which not less than 50% of the period of study taken as a whole shall have been devoted to psychology as a main subject in a degree-granting institution or institutions and shall have completed the requirements for a degree, or shall have obtained an approved postgraduate qualification in psychology awarded by a degree-granting institution, or passed such comprehensive examinations in psychology as shall be approved by the council. A person who shall satisfy the council that he holds such other qualifications as the council may accept may also become an associate member.

Divisions

The three main divisions of the APS are (1) clinical psychology, (2) educational psychology, and (3) occupational psychology.

The membership of the Division of Clinical Psychologists is limited to honorary fellows, fellows, and members of the APS who have been actively engaged in practice, research, teaching, or administration in the field of clinical psychology at least 2 years full time. The members of the clinical division must have completed an approved postgraduate course of supervised training in clinical psychology extending over a period of not less than 1 year full time or its equivalent part time.

The Division of Educational Psychologists admits for membership members of the APS who have, in addition, successfully completed a recognized teacher training course or hold a recognized postgraduate qualification in a field relevant to psychology or have completed 2 years' experience in educational psychology.

The Division of Occupational Psychologists admits members of the APS who are engaged in vocational, personnel, human engineering, organizational, and consumer psychology.

Education and Training

Practically all Australian schools of higher learning offer courses in psychology but only 20 are accredited by the Australian Psychological Society. Most universities offer a 3-year program for students who major in psychology, and a 4th year of "honors."

Thirty-eight schools of higher learning offer a bachelor's degree (B.A., B.Sc., etc.), 9 offer special graduate diplomas (6 in clinical psychology, 3 in other areas), 40 schools of higher learning give master's degrees (M.A., M.Sc., etc.), 19 universities grant the Ph.D. degree.

The Australian Psychological Society exercises a considerable influence on the education of psychologists by setting standards for the accreditation of courses for purposes of membership in the society.

Legal Status

In Australian states there is no governmental supervision of the training in psychology, except in two states, Victoria and South Australia. These two states require registration of psychologists. In order to register, one must hold a university degree in psychology. Other states contemplate similar legislation, although the level of a required degree (e.g., M.A.) is still a controversial issue.

Research

Psychology departments in most universities are well equipped for basic and applied research. A considerable part of the research is devoted to social problems of city and rural life, immigrants, and the aboriginal population. University-based research projects are usually financed by grants from university research funds, the Australian Research Grants Committee, the Australian Advisory Committee for Research and Development in Education, and other sources. Research students are funded through postgraduate awards from the Australian government. There are no private research centers.

Publications

The Australian Psychological Society publishes two journals: the *Australian Journal of Psychology* and the *Australian*

Psychologist. Each journal appears three times per year. The *Australian Psychologist* also publishes monograph supplements.

Australian psychologists frequently write articles and books mostly published in Great Britain and the United States.

Occupational Distribution

There are about 3,000 psychologists in Australia. About one-half of them hold academic positions in universities, teachers' colleges, and so on. Close to 10% of Australian psychologists work in public agencies and hospitals in clinical practice, mostly doing psychodiagnosis. Somewhat fewer than 10% work in the school system, and about an equal number work in vocational psychology, human factor psychology, personnel practices, engineering psychology, organizational psychology, and other fields of industrial psychology. Some psychologists are involved in public health, welfare, and basic and applied research. Some clinical psychologists practice psychology and group psychology, mostly in institutional settings and less frequently in private practice.

Opportunities for Foreign Psychologists

There are no nationwide regulations concerning the rights of foreigners to teach and/or to practice psychology in Australia. Foreign psychologists are advised to address their inquiries and to send their credentials to the Australian Psychological Society at the previously stated address.

Austria[1]

Introduction

The origins of Austrian psychology are linked with great names in the cultural history of mankind. The Austrian capital, Vienna, was for centuries one of the great centers of European thought and science. The search for roots of Austrian psychology leads in several directions, namely, the philosophical-humanistic theories of Brentano and Meinong, the logical-philosophical studies of the Viennese neopositivists (Wiener Kreis), and the medical psychiatric tradition of Krafft-Ebing, Nothnagel, and Brücke that culminated in the works of Sigmund Freud and his disciples.

National Organization

Most Austrian psychologists belong to the German Psychological Association with whom they share a common language and similar training programs. In 1948 the Berufsverband Österreichischer Psychologen (BOP)—the Professional Association of Austrian Psychologists—was formed. At the present time the association has 450 members.

The address of the BOP is:

Berufsverband Österreichischer Psychologen
Liebiggasse 5
1010 Wien
Austria

The official language is German.

[1]Based on information supplied by R. O. Zucha, on behalf of the BOP in Vienna, and other sources.

Internal Structure

The association is governed by (1) the general assembly, (2) the board of directors, (3) a control committee, and (4) a court of arbitration.

The general assembly meets once a year. It can be also convoked at the request of 10 members of the BOP or two members of the council. The main tasks of the general assembly are election of the governing bodies, approval of the reports of the board of directors and the controller's reports, and determination of the overall policy of the BOP.

There are nine directors, all of them elected by a two-thirds majority vote of the general assembly for a 2-year period. The arbitration court is composed of five members, elected in the same manner as the two other governing bodies of the BOP.

Membership

The BOP has 450 members. There are four classes of membership: (1) regular members, (2) temporary members, (3) special members, and (4) honorary members.

Membership Requirements

In order to be admitted to regular membership one must have a Ph.D. in psychology or a diploma in psychology issued by an Austrian or equivalent foreign school of higher learning. The applicants must adduce proof of at least 2 years of successful work in the field of psychology. University professors and docents (assistant professors) of Austrian and equivalent foreign schools of higher learning are admitted to regular membership.

Psychologists who cannot prove their 2 years' experience are admitted to temporary membership until they can provide the required proof.

Holders of Ph.D. degrees in disciplines other than psychology are admitted as special members. Honorary membership can be granted for an exceptional contribution to psychology and/or to the objectives of the BOP.

Major Activities

The BOP holds annual conferences devoted to continuous training and enhancement of psychology as a science and a profession.

Legal Status

Despite the efforts of BOP, there are no laws that would determine the rights and obligations of psychologists in Austria. The BOP has requested that such laws exist and continues its efforts in this direction.

Research

Austrian universities encourage research in various fields of psychology, among them clinical, educational, industrial, and social, often in cooperation with governmental agencies.

Publications

The main journal of Austrian psychologists is the *Wiener Zeitschrift für Philosophie, Psychologie, und Pädagogie*. Austrian psychologists contribute articles and publish books in Germany and in German-speaking Switzerland.

Opportunities for Foreign Psychologists

Austrian universities accept foreign students provided they can, within 1 to 1½ years, pass an examination in German and Latin. Austria participates in student exchange programs with several countries around the world.

Governmental positions in clinical, industrial, and educational psychology as well as regular teaching positions at the universities are open to Austrian citizens only. Psychologists invited to a permanent teaching position automatically receive Austrian citizenship. There are, however, numerous opportunities for temporary and visiting appointments in Austrian universities, hospitals, industry, and government. All inquiries should be addressed to Austrian consulates.

Belgium[1]

Introduction

Psychology in Belgium is a well-established area of study, research, and practice. Psychology is included in the curricula of medical and educational training. As a rule, psychology departments in the universities are associated with departments of education and jointly form an Institute of Psychological and Pedagogical Sciences. These institutes train psychologists in various specialties as well as for teaching assignments in universities and teachers' colleges.

National Organization

The national psychological organization in Belgium is the Belgische Vereniging voor Psychologie—Société Belge de Psychologie. The address of the central office is:

G. d'Ydewalle, Ph.D.
Psychology Department
University of Louvain, B-3000 Louvain
Belgium

The official languages are Dutch and French.

Internal Structure

The executive committee of the Belgian Psychological Society is composed of eleven members: (1) a president, (2) a

[1]Based on information supplied by Dr. G. d'Ydewalle and other sources.

past president, (3) two vice-presidents, (4) two general secretaries, (5) two assistant secretaries, (6) two editors of
Psychologica Belgica, and (7) a treasurer.

Membership

The members of the executive committee are elected every 2 years in a general assembly by the members of the society. There are over 70 full members and about 300 associate
members, a total of about 370. They are divided into three
divisions: (1) general and experimental psychology, (2) developmental and counseling psychology, and (3) social and
professional psychology.

Membership Requirements

Admission requirements for associate members are a university degree in psychology, main professional activities in
the field of psychology, and membership approved by two-
thirds of the general assembly. Full members are required to
have a Ph.D. in psychology plus important activities in
psychology, and full membership approved by two-thirds of the
general assembly.

Major Activities

The organization holds one annual meeting with a number
of lectures, followed by the general assembly; the society also
sponsors the publication of two journals: *Psychologica Belgica*
and *Informatie-Bulletin—Bulletin d'Information.*

Education and Training

Educational facilities consist of a number of schools or
institutes offering training in psychology plus types of degrees
or diplomas. These are described as follows:

Vrije Universiteit te Brussel. Two years of candidatures, followed by 3 years, are required to obtain a license with the following main programs: (1) license in clinical psychology—adults, (2) license in clinical psychology—children and adolescents, (3) license in industrial psychology, and (4) license in experimental psychology.

Rijksuniversiteit Gent. Two years of candidatures, followed by 3 years, are required to obtain a license with the following main programs: (1) developmental and clinical psychology, (2) industrial psychology, (3) theoretical and experimental psychology, and (4) social intervention (youth health/adult education).

Katholieke Universiteit te Leuven. Two years of candidatures, followed by 2 years, are required to obtain a license with the following main programs (3 years are needed for clinical psychology): (1) industrial psychology, (2) school and teaching psychology, (3) experimental and fundamental research, and (4) clinical psychology.

Université Catholique de Louvain. Two years of candidatures, followed by 3 years, are required to obtain a license with the following main programs: (1) general and experimental psychology, (2) differential and clinical psychology, (3) social psychology, and (4) pedagogical psychology.

Université de Liège. Two years of candidatures, followed by 3 years, are required to obtain a license with the following main programs: (1) industrial psychology, (2) guidance and counseling, (3) experimental psychology, and (4) psychology of language.

Université Libre de Bruxelles. Two years of candidatures, followed by 3 years, are required to obtain a license.

The degree of doctor in psychology is attained by only a small number of advanced students and requires the presentation and defense of a thesis based on an original research project. Most students devote approximately 5 or 6 years to their doctoral work.

The average number of students in each degree or diploma program is not available. In 1977−1978 there were 1,100 1st-year students in psychology and educational sciences. In 1977, 300 final degrees in psychology and educational sciences were given.

Governmental Supervisory System for Accreditation

Some studies at Belgian universities give access to a legal degree. For those studies the admission regulation and the study program are legally defined. Studies in psychology give only scientific degrees, not legal degrees. The admission regulation and the study programs are defined by the free universities themselves (Université Libre de Bruxelles, Vrije Universiteit te Brussel, Katholieke Universiteit te Leuven, Université Catholique de Louvain) or by the king in the state universities (Rijksuniversiteit Gent and Université de Liège).

Legal Status

Generally, recognition and professional employment as a psychologist require the completion of a specialized course of study in psychology at a university and the degree of license. However, there is no legal recognition or official registration of psychologists. Graduates of some technical schools with nonuniversity diplomas in psychology or social work are recognized as assistant psychologists or social workers.

A professional ethical code has been proposed but not yet approved by the general assembly of the Belgian Psychological Society.

Research

Most of the psychological research in Belgium is conducted by research centers, laboratories, and clinics affiliated with the departments of psychology in the universities.

The main agency that provides support for research is the

National Foundation for Scientific Research. This foundation supports a large number of pre- and post-doctoral research fellowships.

Publications

The Belgian Psychological Society publishes two journals, mentioned above. There are a few other professional journals as, for example, *Revue de Psychologie et des Sciences de l'Education*. Belgium is a small country and only a few scholarly books are published. They are generally published abroad.

Opportunities for Foreign Psychologists

The knowledge of Dutch and/or French is a prerequisite for any psychological activity in Belgium. There have been rare permanent teaching appointments for foreigners, but there have been opportunities for visiting professorships and research. Applications must be mailed directly to a particular university.

Bolivia[1]

Education and Training

Bolivian schools of higher learning offer courses in psychology. The Catholic University of Bolivia (Universidad Católica Boliviana, U.C.B.) has a department of psychology and psychological careers. This department cooperates with the Minister of Education of Bolivia in preparing school psychologists and guidance workers for governmental educational institutions. The U.C.B. grants the degree of license (licenciado) in psychology, which is a lower level, and the higher degree of superior psychological technician (técnico superior en psicología). There are currently over 300 alumni psychologists who have received the licenciado degree and 40 who hold the superior degree.

The Department of Psychology at San Andrés University (Universidad Mayor de San Andrés) offers courses in psychology, but it does not offer training in professional psychology.

Teachers' colleges (escuelas normales), which train high school teachers, offer training in teaching psychology in high schools.

All instruction in schools of higher learning is conducted in Spanish.

Publications

A bimonthly, *Revista Boliviana de Psicología,* is published by the U.C.B.

[1]Based on information supplied by P. J. Carnibella, professor of psychology, Universidad Católica Boliviana, La Paz, Bolivia, and other sources.

Opportunities for Foreign Psychologists

Foreign psychologists interested in permanent or visiting teaching positions should apply directly to the appropriate university.

Brazil[1]

There are about 8,000 psychologists in Brazil, working in a variety of fields such as clinical, educational, social, industrial, and experimental psychology.

National Organizations

There are in Brazil two national psychological associations; one of them is the Brazilian Psychological Association

Avenida Ipiranga, 345
9° andar, cj. 904 São Paulo, S.P.

This association is affiliated with the International Union of Psychological Science (IUPS). At the present time about 500 psychologists are members of this society.

The other national association is the
Associacão Brasileira de Psicologia Aplicada (APBA)
Praia do Botafogo, 186
s.101 Rio de Janeiro, R. J.

The ABPA derives most of its membership from Rio de Janeiro. The executive body, called the directorate, is elected once in 3 years.

The ABPA admits qualified psychologists to full membership and psychology students to associate membership. The ABPA has 441 full members and 266 associate members.

[1]Based on information supplied by Prof. Arrigo Leonardo Angelini, president of the Federal Council of Psychology (Conselho Federal de Psicologia) and Dr. Franco Lo Presti Seminério, president of the Brazilian Association of Applied Psychology (Associacão Brasileira de Psicologia Aplicada).

The oldest regional psychological association in Brazil, founded in 1945, is the Psychological Society of São Paulo, with a membership of approximately 400 psychologists. Students of psychology may also join this society as affiliate members. The number of student members is considerable, around 600.
More recent regional associations are:

Mineiran Society of Psychology
Avenida Amazonas, 135
s. 807 Belo Horizonte, M.G.

Psychological Society of Rio Grande do Sul
Rua Otavio Rocha, 116
cj. 61 Pôrto Alegre, RGS

Professional Association of Psychologists of Guanabara
Praia do Botafogo, 186
2° grupo, Rio de Janeiro

Pernambucan Association of Psychologists
Rua Costa Gomes, 129
Recife, Pernambuco

Bahian Association of Psychologists
Rua Francisco Ferraro, 17
Salvador, Bahia

Psychological Society of Federal District, SCS
Edificio Sonia
s. 304 Brasilia, D.V.

Psychological Society of Ribeirão Pretô
Caixa postal 1006
Ribeirão Pretô

Besides these regional psychological organizations, there are certain societies that deal with special fields; among them are:

Rorschach Society of São Paulo
Avenida Santo Amaro, 62
São Paulo, S.P.

Brazilian Society of Psychoanalysis of Rio de Janeiro
Rua 19 de Fevereiro. no. 17
Rio de Janeiro, R.J.

Brazilian Society of Psychoanalysis of São Paulo
Rua Itacolomi, 601
8º andar São Paulo, S.P.

Brazilian Society of Religious Psychology
Rua Monte Alegre, 984
São Paulo, S.P.

There is, in addition, one psychologists' union:

Sindicato dos Psicologos
No Estado de São Paulo
Avenida Brigadeiro Luis Antonio, 4187
São Paulo, S.P.

Education and Training

Sixty-two Brazilian universities offer courses in psychology. Thirty-five hundred students are annually admitted to these and undergraduate courses. The organization of university studies follows the law on Directives and Bases of National Education (1961). According to this law, the duration and the minimum curriculum for each program of study must be set by the Federal Council of Education and required duration and minimum curriculum must be the same for all universities and schools of higher education throughout the country.

University psychology programs are set for at least 5 years of study with a minimum of 4,050 hours of academic work. This minimum duration is usually surpassed by the schools of higher learning.

As far as the content is concerned, the following courses ask the minimum requirement: physiology, statistics, general and experimental psychology, developmental psychology, psychology of personality, social psychology, psychopathology, psychological testing and counseling, and professional ethics. Besides these subjects, the university must specify three additional courses from the following list: psychology of exceptional children, group dynamics and human relations, educational therapeutics, educational psychology and problems of learning, theories and techniques of psychotherapy, personnel selection, and industrial psychology. The above is the required minimum curriculum, but each school must add other courses in order to establish the so-called full curriculum.

Frequently, courses like biology, neurology, anatomy, sociology, anthropology, philosophy, psychology of learning, comparative psychology, psycholinguistics, special psychotherapy, and projective techniques are included in the requirements by the school, according to the local interests and possibilities.

The minimum curriculum required for the title of psychologist includes at least 500 additional hours of supervised training in various areas of applied psychology, usually clinical, educational, or industrial.

Advanced Training. This additional training may take place outside the university at private or public institutions that have appropriate facilities, but almost all the universities offering programs in psychology also have clinics and/or centers of applied psychology with provision for training students.

By the end of the 1960s, the Brazilian universities experienced a substantial reform in their structures and the old system of chairs (catedras) was changed into the new system of departments, in a way more or less similar to that of the American universities. With this reform the basic training of the psychologists did not undergo much change.

However, at the postgraduate level, in the late 1970s, some universities established courses leading to master's and doctoral degrees with programs of studies and credits that are very similar to those prevalent in graduate courses at the American universities.

This postgraduate training is structured in terms of major courses (concentration areas) and complementary courses. The major areas are school psychology, clinical psychology, social psychology, experimental psychology, and industrial psychology.

For the time being, only six institutions offer such advanced programs. The Institute of Psychology, State University of São Paulo, offers master's and doctoral programs with majors in the areas of psychology of school children and experimental psychology and also master programs with majors in clinical psychology and social psychology. Up to now, the State University of São Paulo is the only Brazilian university that offers doctoral programs in psychology. São Paulo offers master's programs with majors in educational psychology and social psychology. In 1978, this institute started a program in clinical psychology.

The Department of Psychology of the Pontifical Catholic University of Rio de Janeiro offers master's programs with majors in social psychology and clinical psychology. The Institute of Vocational Selection and Guidance of the Getulio Vargas Foundation in Rio de Janeiro offers master's programs with majors in industrial psychology, personnel selection, and ergonomics.

The University Gama Filho in Rio de Janeiro offers master's programs in the areas of school psychology and theoretical psychology.

The Institute of Psychology of the Pontifical Catholic University of Rio Grande do Sul offers master's programs in applied psychology.

The Department of Psychology of the Pontifical Catholic University of Campinas, State of São Paulo, offers a master's program in clinical psychology. The Department of Psychology, University of Brasilia, offers master's programs in the areas of clinical psychology and the psychology of school children.

In 1977 the Department of Psychology, Federal University of Pernambuco, in Recife City, started a master's program in cognitive psychology.

In Brazilian universities, lectures are generally in Portuguese with the exception of courses delivered by visiting professors at the postgraduate levels. Theses and dissertations must also be written in Portuguese.

Legal Status

The psychological profession has been recognized by law in Brazil since August 27, 1962, when Federal Law No. 4119 was sanctioned by the president of the country after a long period of discussion and the final approval of the national congress.

According to this law the title of psychologist is applicable to persons who have completed a regular university course, with the curriculum and training described in the section on education and training.

Before the existence of that law, psychological practice was in the hands of professionals trained overseas and those who, having completed a university course in the fields of education, philosophy, and social sciences, had received additional on-the-job training in private or public institutions or had had postgraduate training in psychology.

The 1962 law established the minimum requirements for the training of psychologists in schools of psychology at the universities, the professional rights of those who have graduated in those schools, the validation of courses taken abroad, and the registration of the professionals at the Ministry of Education.

The law established that an exclusive prerogative of the psychologist is to utilize psychological methods and techniques with the following purposes: (1) psychological diagnosis, (2) occupational selection and guidance, (3) psychoeducational guidance, and (4) solution of adjustment problems.

As a consequence of this law that recognized the profession of psychologist as independent and then established requirements, there was a rapid expansion in training programs in psychology in many universities, paralleled with the growing interest in psychology on the part of young students seeking a higher education. At the present time, psychology is one of the subjects most chosen by those entering the Brazilian universities.

Federal Council

In December of 1971 another important federal law was approved concerning the psychological profession. This law created the Federal Council of Psychology and the Regional Councils of Psychology as official organizations, administratively and financially autonomous, whose purposes are to direct, discipline, and supervise the psychological profession.

Two years after the approval of this new law, the first federal council was elected by an assembly of about 40 delegates from the psychological associations, and this council was installed under the auspices of the Ministry of Labor. The Federal Council of Psychology is composed of nine effective members and nine substituting members, all psychologists in full professional rights.

The central office of this council is located in Brasilia; the address is:

> Conselho Federal de Psicologia—SCS
> Edificio Arnaldo Villares, Salas 203/4
> CEP 70.000
> Brasilia, South America

Besides the responsibilities of the Federal Council of Psychology, such as directing, disciplining, and supervising the profession all over the country, this council establishes the ethical code of the profession and functions as a federal tribunal of the psychologists who violate such a code. The council also determines the legal limits of professional activities.

Regional Councils

In April 1974 the council divided Brazil into seven regions and organized the Regional Councils of Psychology (Conselhos Regionais de Psicologia) as follows:

1st Region. CRP-01, with the central office in Brasilia City, including Brasilia D.F., the states of Acre, Amazonas,

Goiás, and Pará, and the federal territories of Amapá, Roraima, and Rondônia.

2nd Region. CRP-02, with the central office in Recife City, including the States of Alagoas, Ceará, Maranhão, Paraíba, Pernambuco, Piauí, and Rio Grande do Norte, and the federal territory of Fernando de Noronha.

3rd Region. CRP-03, with the central office in Salvador City, including the states of Bahia and Sergipe.

4th Region. CRP-04, with the central office in Belo Horizonte City, including the states of Espírito Santo and Minas Gerais.

5th Region. CRP-05, with the central office in Rio de Janeiro, including the state of Rio de Janeiro.

6th Region. CRP-06, with the central office in São Paulo, including the states of Mato Grosso and São Paulo.

7th Region. CRP-07, with the central office in Pôrto Alegre, including the states of Paraná, Rio Grande do Sul, and Santa Catarina.

Registration

The regional councils register all psychologists working in their respective geographical region. This registration is compulsory and no psychologist is allowed to practice without it. The regional council has almost the same responsibilities as the federal council, in its respective region only, and its members are the individual psychologists, whereas in the case of the federal council the membership is represented by the seven regional councils.

Each psychologist has to pay an annual fee to his regional council, and one-third of the income of each regional council constitutes the budget of the federal council.

Every 3 years elections are held. At the regional level there are general elections to fill the offices. At the federal level, two delegates of each regional council meet in Brasilia in order to elect the new officers of the next federal council.

In order to be registered as a psychologist in a regional council one must present a diploma of graduation in psychology from an official university or a private one approved by the Ministry of Education.

Those psychologists who were trained before the 1962 law may present, instead of the diploma, a document proving that they met the requirements of professional transitional registration at the Ministry of Education. They must prove that they worked as psychologists for at least 5 years or had at least 2 years of postgraduate training.

Research

The National Institute of Educational Research and Studies of the Brazilian government offers grants for research in psychology. The Getulio Vargas Foundation supports research in applied psychology.

Research activities are being carried out mainly in those universities that offer postgraduate courses. The laboratories at the other universities have been used primarily for teaching. It is mainly in the following institutes or departments that research programs in psychology are carried out.

Institute of Psychology, State University of São Paulo. Here the research interests include specific problems in learning, the psychology of childhood and adolescence, psychological testing and other psychometric techniques, motivation, personality problems and techniques, and cross-cultural research of childhood and adolescence.

There are, in addition, research programs on problems of social psychology, mental deficiency, animal learning, and sensation and perception.

Institute of Psychology, Pontifical Catholic University of São Paulo. In this institution the research projects include the psychology of adolescence and social psychology, parent—child relationships in clinical psychology, test construction, studies of various aspects of personality structure, cross-cultural studies on personality, and investigations of the effects of variations in cultural variables on perceptual learning and on the physiological aspects of behavior. **Department of Psychology, Pontifical Catholic University of Rio de Janeiro.** Research centers mainly on adolescent and social psychology, clinical psychology and test construction, personality, and psychophysiology, as well as learning and motivation. **Department of Psychology, University of Minas Gerais.** Research work is being done in social psychology, student selection procedures, and projective techniques. **Institute of Psychology, Pontifical Catholic University of Rio Grande do Sul.** Research is being done in problems of personality, test construction, social psychology, and human development. **Department of Psychology, University of Brasilia.** Here, research is conducted on teaching methods and program instruction, decision making as influenced by sensory processes, delay of reinforcement in children, schedules of reinforcement, and other problems in the learning area. **Department of Psychology, University of São Paulo in Ribeirão Prêto.** Research interests include problems of learning and reinforcement and open space perception.

It should be added that none of these institutions is concerned exclusively with research; teaching is generally the major occupation of their staff members.

Publications

Reports of research works are published in a few publications devoted exclusively to psychological matters and some other journals that include papers in various scientific fields.

The main journals are *Brazilian Archives of Applied Psychology* (ISOP Rua da Candelaria no. 6, Rio de Janeiro), the *Bulletin of Psychology* (Psychological Society of São Paulo), and the *Review of Normal and Abnormal Psychology*

(Pontifical Catholic University of São Paulo). Most of the psychological associations also have regular publications. The *Review of the Brazilian Society for the Advancement of Science* has a section for psychological papers. The Catholic University of Rio Grande do Sul publishes the journal *Psyco.*

Opportunities for Foreign Psychologists

Brazilian universities welcome foreign psychologists for temporary or permanent teaching positions, provided they can teach in Portuguese. Applications should be addressed directly to the respective university; the addresses can be obtained from any Brazilian consulate.

In order to practice clinical or another applied psychology, the foreign psychologist must obtain a Brazilian validation of his diploma. The validation takes a long time and, in some cases, an additional training period in a Brazilian university is required. Inquiries should be addressed to the

Conselho Federal de Psicologia
Edificio Arnaldo Vilares, Sala 408
Setor Commercial Sul
Brasilia, D.F.
Brazil

Bulgaria[1]

National Organization

All 250 Bulgarian psychologists are members of the national Bulgarian Psychological Society established in 1962. The address of the society is:

> 1000 Sofia C
> P.O.B. 1333
> Bulgaria

Internal Structure

The central governing body of the society, called the Bureau, is composed of president, vice-president, secretary, treasurer, and presidents of sections. The society has five divisions, namely: (1) general psychology, (2) social psychology, (3) child psychology, (4) medical (clinical) psychology, and (5) psychology of labor and engineering. The society has regional branches all over the country. The Society of Sportive Psychology and the Student Psychological Society are affiliated with the governing body of the Bulgarian Psychological Society. The bureau is elected at the annual plenary session of all members of the society.

Membership

In addition to the regular, full members, there are 23 student members (Student Psychological Society). The members

[1]Based on information supplied by Dogomil Velichkov, cultural attaché, Embassy of the People's Republic of Bulgaria, Washington, D.C., and other sources.

of the society must have high university degrees in philosophy, pedagogy, or psychology; they are expected to conduct research in psychology. Student members must have high marks in their university studies and take active part in research and, preferably, have published scholarly articles.

Major Activities

The Bulgarian Psychological Society holds national conferences. The I and II National Conferences were devoted to psychology in the different fields and to the coming tasks. The III National Conference was devoted to the social-psychological climate in schools, work, scientific bodies, military, etc. In addition, the society conducts a permanent seminar on psychological problems and stands in close contact with national organizations on psychology in other countries.

Education and Training

The faculty of philosophy of the University of Ochridski in Sofia offers professional training in psychology. The Sofia university grants the following degrees: (1) candidate of psychological sciences (psychology), (2) candidate of philosophical sciences (philosophy), (3) doctor of psychological sciences.

There are 40 students in advanced psychological studies.

The training of psychologists and the nature of the final examination for obtaining degrees are determined by the government, which issues rules and regulations concerning the conferring of scientific degrees and titles.

The professional ethics and the disciplinary procedures are determined by the governmental labor code, the constitution of the Bulgarian Psychological Society, and the statutes of the Student Psychological Society.

Research

All Bulgarian universities actively engage in research in various fields of psychology. The Laboratory of Psychology of

the Bulgarian Academy of Sciences has a special Research Institute in education and educational psychology. The Bulgarian
Academy of Medical Sciences, the Sofia Medical Institute, and
the Central Pediatric Institute engage in research in
psychopathology, diagnostics, and therapy. The staff of the
Chair of Psychology of the University of Ochridski in Sofia
conducts research in developmental, educational, and industrial psychology. The Central Institute for Postgraduate Study of
Teachers, the staff of the Chair of Psychology in Pedagogical
Institutes conducts research in child psychology. The Institute
of Physical Culture engages in psychological studies of athle-
tics.

Publications

The Bulgarian Psychological Society publishes a journal,
Psychology. This journal prints psychological studies.
Psychological research is also reported in the journal, *People's
Education,* and in yearbooks of the institutions for graduate
and postgraduate studies. Psychological studies are often included in *Proceedings of the Research Institute for Education,
Proceedings of the High Institute for Physical Culture,* and *Proceedings of the Institute for Pediatrics.* The entire instruction
and all publications are in the Bulgarian language.

Opportunities for Foreign Psychologists

Foreign psychologists wishing to visit Bulgaria must apply
to the Bulgarian consular services.

Canada[1]

National Organization

The Canadian Psychological Association (Société Canadienne de Psychologie) has about 2,000 members, and conducts its affairs in English and French. Its address is:

> Canadian Psychological Association
> Siège Social
> Department of Psychology
> University of Toronto
> Toronto, Ontario
> Canada

The aims of the Canadian Psychological Association are:

to promote by discussion and research and dissemination of information the advancement and practical application of psychological studies in Canada; to issue such publications as may from time to time be considered necessary and feasible; to render such assistance as it can to governments and other organizations concerned with education, health, administration of justice, industry, national defense, and other social and national problems; to do and conduct such activities as may be considered necessary to forward the objects of the Association; to receive, hold and use all money and other property in any manner acquired for the benefit of the Association.

Internal Structure

The affairs of the association are managed by a board of directors. The board shall consist of (1) the immediate past

[1]Based on information supplied by Charles Roger Myers, executive officer of the Canadian Psychological Association, and other sources.

president, (2) the president, (3) the president-elect, (4) the chairmen of the applied and experimental divisions, and (5) six other directors, two being elected each year for a term of 3 years by the fellows and members of the association.

The board of directors elects a small executive committee composed of (1) the immediate past president, (2) the president, (3) the president-elect, (4) the two directors who are in the 3rd year of their term, and (5) the secretary-treasurer and the executive officer.

Membership

There are four classes of membership:

Fellows. Fellows shall be members of the association who have made a distinguished contribution to the advancement of the science or profession of psychology or who have given exceptional service to their national or provincial associations.

Members. Applicants for membership must possess a master's degree in psychology, or its academic equivalent, conferred by a graduate school of recognized standing.

Honorary Life Fellows and Members. At age 65, fellows and members who have been members of the association for at least 15 years shall continue as fellows and members without payment of fees and shall be known as "honorary life fellows" or "honorary life members," as the case may be. The board of directors may, at its discretion, confer honorary life status on any fellow or member on his retirement.

Honorary Fellows. Honorary fellows shall be distinguished members of other disciplines or psychologists whom the association wishes to honor for their contribution to Canadian psychology. They may be elected at any meeting of the board of directors by a three-quarters vote of the directors present at such meeting. Honorary fellows shall not be eligible to vote or hold office in the association.

In addition, the association admits student affiliates and foreign affiliates.

Education and Training

Fifty-eight Canadian universities offer training in psychology, and 41 of these offer advanced training. Thirteen universities grant master's degrees, and 28 have doctoral programs in psychology. The most diversified and extensive programs in psychology are offered by McGill University in Montreal (in English), University of Alberta in Edmonton (in English), University of Toronto (in English), University of Montreal (in French), University of Ottawa (in French and English), and the University of Western Ontario in London, Ontario (in English).

Legal Status

The practice of psychology in Canada is regulated by laws issued by the individual provinces, in cooperation with the provincial psychological associations. There are 10 provinces in Canada; 6 of them have statutory registration boards (New Brunswick, Quebec, Ontario, Manitoba, Saskatchewan, Alberta) and 1 nonstatutory (British Columbia).

Research

Canadian universities encourage faculty members and advanced students to conduct research in practically every field of psychology. Most of them are well equipped and operate their own laboratories, and some of them also operate clinics. The Canadian government and some provinces have their own research programs related to defense, public health, education, and so on. Support for research can be obtained from the National Research Council, the Medical Research Council, and the Canada Council, as well as private sources.

Publications

The Canadian Psychological Association publishes three quarterly journals, listed below. Each journal publishes articles in both English and French and has a circulation of between one and two thousand.

The *Canadian Psychologist,* published in January, April, July, and October, is a journal of general psychology including interpretive, theoretical, discipline bridging, and mission scholarship, evaluative reviews, comment on psychological affairs and organizational psychology, and original research having technological importance.

The *Canadian Journal of Psychology* published in March, June, September, and December, publishes experimental and theoretical articles in all recognized fields of psychology.

The *Canadian Journal of Behavioural Science* published in January, April, July, and October, publishes articles in the applied areas of psychology and both research and theoretical articles in the areas of social, personality, abnormal, educational, and developmental and child psychology.

Opportunities for Foreign Psychologists

Canadian universities welcome foreign teachers and research workers. However, there are no uniform nationwide rules concerning opportunities for foreign psychologists, and each province sets its own rules and regulations.

Foreign psychologists interested in temporary or permanent teaching positions or any other job in Canada should address themselves either to the Canadian Psychological Association, or to one of the 10 provincial associations, or to a particular university.

Chile[1]

National Organization

Most Chilean psychologists belong to their national organization, the

Colegio de Psicólogos de Chile
Londres 84, Departamento 2
Santiago, Chile
The official language is Spanish.

Internal Structure

The ruling body of the *colegio* (the national organization) is the *consejo general* (general council) with nine members—namely, the president, vice-president, treasurer, secretary, and five counselors.

Membership Requirements

To be admitted to membership, one must be in possession of a professional degree in psychology issued by a Chilean university or a foreign equivalent.

Major Activities

The aims of the colegio are (1) to secure progress and prestige for the profession as well as to supervise and discipline

[1]Based on information supplied by Liana Ortiz Wolf, president of the Colegio de Psicólogos de Chile; Dr. Hernán Berwart Torrens, director of the School of Psychology of the Universidad Católica de Chile; and other sources.

the proper professional conduct, (2) to encourage national and international research, and (3) to cooperate with public and private universities. The colegio holds annual meetings in April.

Education and Training

Two Chilean universities, La Universidad de Chile and La Universidad Católica de Chile, offer a professional degree of psychology. In order to obtain this degree the students must fulfill course requirements, undergo a prescribed practicum, write a thesis, and pass final examinations. Thirty-four students are admitted annually to the two psychology departments.

Legal Status

The degree granted by the University of Chile is tantamount to legal recognition and admits to teaching and practice.

Research

The colegio and the two universities encourage their faculty members and advanced students to engage in research.

Publications

The national association (colegio) publishes the *Boletín Informativo* (Information Bulletin) in Spanish.

Occupational Distribution

Among the 514 members of the colegio, 279 are clinical psychologists, 54 are industrial psychologists, 42 are educational psychologists, and 16 are social psychologists.

Opportunities for Foreign Psychologists

Foreign psychologists who seek employment in Chile must have their degree validated by a Chilean university.

China[1]

Introduction

For centuries, Chinese intellectuals have been under the influence of the psychological concepts of Hinduism, Buddhism, Confucianism, and Taoism. The secret book of Upanishads has described four mental states, two of them unconscious and two conscious. Sleeping and dreaming were believed to be unconscious, while waking and meditation were conscious. The latter state represented the highest level of awareness, reaching a total tranquillity and inner harmony. One of these states is the Yoga.

The 19th century and the first half of the 20th century brought Western influences, and many wealthy Chinese sent their sons to study in Europe and the United States. The psychologies of Wundt, Külpe, Stern, and others, and the American theories of Titchener, James, Dewey, and others have influenced the Chinese. In the first five decades of the 20th century, the American influence was rapidly growing, and several Chinese universities used American textbooks in psychology.

In 1949, with the establishment of the communist People's Republic of China, the philosophical teachings of Marx and Lenin and the Russian psychology of Pavlov had become the only avenue of research, teaching, and practice. Several works by USSR psychologists had been translated into Chinese, and Russian psychology dominated Chinese universities.

[1]Based on information supplied by various sources.

National Organization

All Chinese psychologists are members of the Chinese Psychological Association, formed in 1955 under the auspices of the central government in Peking. The main aim of the association is to serve the Chinese nation in its efforts to build a Marxist society. Chinese psychologists, and all other scientists in the People's Republic of China alike, are socially conscious workers of the republic, and all their activities aim at goals serving the "New Man." The Marxist concepts of human behavior and the governmental goals of building the new social system are the guideposts of research, teaching, and practice of Chinese psychologists.

Education and Training

Several senior Chinese psychologists have received their training in Europe and in the United States. Chinese psychologists are trained in the Chinese universities, whose curriculum reflects Western influences and Marxism. All of them stress the social responsibilities of psychologists in developing communism.

Research

Scientific research is conducted by the Institute of Psychology of the Chinese Academy of Science in Peking and by several universities.

Publications

The two main journals of the Chinese psychologists are *Acta Psychologica Sinica* and *Problems of Psychology*. The first journal publishes research papers as well as programmatic articles pointing to the political tasks of Chinese psychologists. The latter journal publishes translations of scientific works in other languages.

Books in psychology combine some old, traditional Chinese concepts of mental health with contemporary conditioning theories.

Occupational Distribution

A great many Chinese psychologists are employed in mental hospitals and clinics, where they cooperate with psychiatrists. Several psychologists are involved in industry and education. There is no private practice.

Opportunities for Foreign Psychologists

Foreign psychologists wishing to visit the People's Republic of China should contact Chinese consular authorities.

Colombia[1]

National Organization

Out of the 1,000 psychologists in Colombia, close to 700 belong to the Colombian Federation of Psychology. The address of the federation is:

Federación Colombiana de Psicología
Apartado Aéreo 5253
Bogotá, Colombia
South America

This national organization is one of the earliest and best established in Latin America. The official language is Spanish.

Internal Structure

According to the statutes of the federation (Article 23), the functions of the executive council are (1) to assume responsibility for the fulfillment of the statutes and propose all changes; (2) to expel or suspend, according to established limitations, any member who breaks the statutes; (3) to approve the divisions and other groups formed in the federation; (4) to nominate the permanent or temporary committees considered pertinent to the attainment of its goals; and (5) to approve applications for membership, if the applicant fulfills all requirements.

In order to achieve the goals of the federation, the executive council organizes seminars, lectures, and the exchange of

[1]Based on information supplied by Rubén Ardilla, Colombian Federation of Psychology, representative to the International Union of Psychological Science, and other sources.

48

information, psychological materials, publications, and anything else related to the improvement of the scientific level of the members and the recognition of professional psychology in Colombia. The executive council also appoints the honors tribunal, which judges any violation of the ethical code of the federation.

Membership

The total number of members is 700, divided into professionals (500) and students (200).

Divisions

The federation has six divisions as follows: (1) experimental psychology, (2) social psychology, (3) industrial psychology, (4) clinical psychology, (5) educational and school psychology, and (6) experimental analysis of behavior.

Membership Requirements

The admissions requirements for the divisions vary. Usually, the divisions require the degree of "psychologist." In some cases, they may require an original paper, relevant to the area of work of the division to which the person is applying.

Major Activities

The major activities of the federation are:

Annual Meetings. Colombian conventions of psychology are held every year; the 1976 convention was the seventh.

Special Conferences. Lectures, seminars, etc., are held.

Representation. Psychology is represented as a science and as a profession to the general public.

Publication. The federation publishes a newsletter, *Boletín*.

Education and Training

Psychological training in Colombia started in 1948 (at the National University), compared with 1950 in Mexico, 1954 in Brazil, and 1958 in Argentina. The following schools offer training in psychology: National University of Colombia (Bogotá), Javeriana University (Bogotá), University of the Andes (Bogotá), University of St. Buenaventúra (Medellín), University of the North (Barranquilla). All five universities grant the degree of psychologist after a 5-year professional training program, similar to the training of engineers, architects, economists, etc. The University of the Andes has a master's degree program, leading to the title of master of psychology (maestro en Psicología).

There are approximately 300 students, in each program, with a total of 1,500 psychology students in the country.

The Colombian Federation of Psychology is very active in the educational system. It controls the growth of the psychology departments and tries to limit the number of psychologists in order to maintain a favorable employment situation; at the present time there are more jobs than psychologists.

Legal Status

The diploma of psychologist is the only prerequisite for working in Colombia. The psychologists are required to register with the Colombian government. The Colombian Federation of Psychology has issued a code of ethics.

Research

Government Agencies. Colciencias, the Colombian government agency that financially supports the sciences, includes psychology among its priorities. The University of the Andes and the University of the North are the ones that give the greatest support to psychological research. In all the others, some support is obtainable.

The Colombian Neurological Institute supports research in physiological psychology. Some support is also available from other private centers.

Publications

The Colombian Federation of Psychology publishes a monthly newsletter, *Boletín*. The other professional journal is the *Revista Latinoamericana de Psicología* (Latin American Journal of Psychology), published three times a year. Its address is:

Revista Latinoamericana de Psicología
Apartado Aéreo 28454
Bogotá, Colombia
South America

Occupational Distribution

Colombian psychologists are involved in research, teach in universities, and work as school psychologists, guidance and vocational counselors, and clinical psychologists in hospitals and other health institutions. Many of them occupy governmental positions. Some clinical psychologists are in private practice.

Opportunities for Foreign Psychologists

Colombia welcomes foreign psychologists for a variety of jobs. For information, one should write to the Federación Colombiana de Psicología at the address given above.

Cuba[1]

National Organization

The national organization that is active at the moment is the
    Sociedad Cubana de Psicología de la Salud
    Edificio del Consejo Científico
    Calle 23 #201
    3 piso
    Vedado, La Habana, Cuba
The official language of the sociedad is Spanish.

Membership Requirements

The sociedad accepts as members psychologists who possess either a licenciado en psicología degree or a Ph.D. in psychology.

Education and Training

There are two training institutes in Cuba. One of them is the Escuela de Psicología of the University of Havana and the other is at the Universidad Central de las Villas. Training takes 5 years and all students receive a thorough training in all areas of scientific and applied psychology.

[1]Based on information supplied by Gerardo Marín, secretary general of the Sociedad Interamericana de Psicología (SIP).

Legal Status

The Cuban government recognizes holders of a licenciado or a Ph.D. as psychologists.

Research and Publications

Research is mostly carried on at the two training institutes and at the large clinical settings, principally the Hospital Psiquiátrico de la Habana. The same hospital publishes *Revista del Hospital Psiquiátrico de la Habana,* which contains mostly clinical and psychiatric papers, with a few general psychological studies. The Ministry of Education publishes the journal *Educación y Psicología* (resumed in 1975 after a long time), directed mainly at applications of psychology to the processes of education and special education.

Occupational Distribution

Psychologists work mainly as clinical psychologists or as diagnosticians for psychiatrists, as school psychologists, as teachers, and also in applied social psychology. The most developed areas seem to be clinical and educational psychology.

Opportunities for Foreign Psychologists

Foreign psychologists interested in teaching in Cuba should apply directly to Cuban universities.

Cyprus[1]

National Organization

There is no national psychological association in Cyprus; this is because until 1970 there was only one trained psychologist in the country. As of 1978, Cyprus claimed only a few fully trained psychologists, probably no more than 30.

It should be noted, however, that there does exist the Cyprus Mental Health Association, whose objective is the promotion of mental health principles on the island; the existing trained psychologists in Cyprus are active members of this association.

Education and Training

The psychologists in Cyprus (two employed as clinical psychologists in the Mental Health Services of the Ministry of Health and two as educational psychologists in the Ministry of Education) are graduates of universities and other higher institutions of European countries. They are usually members of the national psychological associations of the countries in which they studied and trained (e.g., British Psychological Society, American Psychological Association, etc.).

There are no schools or institutions in Cyprus offering training in psychology. Since there is no national psychological organization, any influence on the educational system came

[1]Based on information supplied by V. P. Vassilopoulos, director general, Ministry of Health, Republic of Cyprus, and other sources.

from the work of individual psychologists or the work of the Cyprus Mental Health Association. In this respect, special facilities for special groups of children were established through the initiative of the Cyprus Mental Health Association and in close cooperation with governmental agencies or through the work of individual psychologists. The work of this voluntary organization and its active members of the mental health specialties has extended into many areas of education and has influenced educational methods, attitudes, and educational organization in many respects.

Legal Status

There are no specific licensing or certification requirements and procedures for the employment of psychologists in Cyprus. Eligibility for employment, however, in the government services (clinical psychologists) requires one to possess a degree in psychology (B.A. Hon.) or B.Sc. or an equivalent diploma from a recognized university and the appropriate postgraduate clinical training in this discipline.

Regarding professional ethical codes and disciplinary procedures, the official psychologists follow the ones that have been in use by relevant psychological associations abroad of which they are members (ethical code of the American Psychological Association, British Psychological Society, etc.).

Research

Research was undertaken by the Cyprus Mental Health Association in such areas as vocational guidance, psychological disturbances in the student population, and other social problems. Individual psychologists have engaged in past research in the areas of mental retardation, standardization of tests, etc.

Publications

Some books on special psychological themes were published either by individual psychologists or by the Cyprus

Mental Organization. Among these are *Mental Health Problems* (1970), *Mental Handicaps in Cyprus* (1973), and *The Guidance of the School Child* (1963).

The Cyprus Mental Health Association, in cooperation with the Educational Research Association, publishes a journal for parents every 3 months.

Occupational Distribution

There are 4 school psychologists and 9 clinical psychologists; 2 psychologists with no special training are employed in other areas, 1 as a teacher, and another as a nurse. There are some 15 Cypriot psychologists employed in different countries abroad.

Opportunities for Foreign Psychologists

These opportunities are rather limited. Inquiries should be addressed to the Ministry of Health, Republic of Cyprus, Nicosia, Cyprus.

Czechoslovakia[1]

National Organization

All the Czech and Slovak psychologists in the Czechoslovak Socialist Republic belong to the

Psychological Association of Czechoslovakia
Prl. Ceskoslovensko Akademii Ved
Náhrězï B., Engelse 6
12800 Praha
Czechoslovakia

The official languages are Czech and Slovak.

The Slovak psychologists have their own association affiliated with the Czechoslovak association. The Slovak association has a considerable degree of independence, especially since 1968.

Membership

Since all degrees are issued by the government, holders of the promovany psycholog, candidate or doctoral degrees, are admitted to membership in the association.

The total number of members is over 500.

Education and Training

The Charles University in Prague was founded in 1348 and was the first university in Central Europe. In 1919 the

[1]Based on information supplied by various sources.

Masaryk University was opened in Brno and the Komenský (Comenius) University in Bratislava. During World War II, Czechoslovakia was under Nazi occupation and all high schools and universities were closed. In 1976 Czechoslovakia had five universities in Prague, Brno, Bratislava, Olomuc, and Kosice. All these universities offer courses in various fields of psychology; all of them have separate psychology departments and laboratories. After 5 years of study, students must pass a state examination, for which they receive the diploma. **Promovany Psycholog.** If students continue their studies and take the additional examination in a specialized area of psychological research or practice, they receive the degree of candidate of science (psychology). An additional 2 years and a dissertation are required for the doctor of science (psychology) degree.

Czechoslovak psychologists receive training in general, experimental, developmental, cognitive, and social psychology. The applied fields include clinical, educational, and industrial psychology. Czechoslovak psychology is influenced by Pavlov's work and Marx–Lenin philosophy.

Research

All training and research programs are operated by governmental agencies. The Czechoslovak Academy of Sciences and the Department of Educational Psychology of its Pedagogical Institute engage in basic research in developmental and educational psychology. The Slovak Academy of Science in Bratislava and its Institute of Experimental Psychology are involved in the study of cognitive processes, human engineering, and neurophysiology. The Psychiatry Institute of the Czechoslovak Ministry of Health is concerned with neurosurgery, psychopathology, and treatment methods.

All universities are research-oriented. The Charles University in Prague conducts research in experimental, social, clinical, and industrial psychology. The Comenius University in Bratislava is involved in research in experimental, comparative, and educational fields, and vocational guidance.

Publications

The Czechoslovak Psychological Association publishes the *News,* and the Slovak association publishes the *Bulletin.* An annual bibliography of psychological literature is published by the Czechoslovak State Library.

Occupational Distribution

All Czechoslovak psychologists are governmental employees, serving as university teachers, researchers, guidance counselors, industrial psychologists, and clinicians.

Opportunities for Foreign Psychologists

Foreign psychologists wishing to visit Czechoslovakia for the sake of research or giving lectures must contact a Czechoslovak consulate.

Denmark[1]

National Organization

The national psychological association of Denmark is the Dansk Psykologforening (Danish Psychological Association)
Sct. Pedersstraede 34–36
DK 1453 København K.
The official language is Danish (correspondence in English, German, or French).

Internal Structure

The board of directors (bestyrelse) is composed of 11 members: president, vice-president, six senior members, and three junior members. The daily activities of the association are conducted by the executive committee (forretningsudvalg), which has four members: president, vice-president, and two members from the board. The standing committees (fast hdvalg) are composed of the following: (1) committee of ethics: five members, chosen at the general assembly for 4 years; (2) committee of judging: four members, chosen at the general assembly for 2 years, evaluates candidates to certain leading positions within the applied area; (3) committee of educational matters: six members, chosen by the board of directors and chaired by one member of the board; (4) committee of financial affairs: chosen by the board and chaired by a board

[1]Based on information supplied by Hans Weltzer, on behalf of the Danish Psychological Association, and other sources.

member. Other committees, headed by a board member elected by the board, are the committees on (1) social policy, (2) unemployment, (3) legislation for psychologists, (4) annual convention, (5) information for members and nonmembers. The association also has several subcommittees.

Membership

The total number of members is as follows: senior members (candidates)—900; junior members (students)—500. Divisions of the association fall into the following categories: (1) clinical psychology, (2) school psychology, (3) education in psychology for nonpsychologists, (4) labor and organizational psychology, (5) county sections (all psychologists in a county or region).

Membership Requirements

The admission requirements for senior members are a completed university degree in psychology, after graduation (candidates of psychology, educational psychology, M.A.); for junior members, that they be students of psychology.

Major Activities

The association acts as a labor union for psychologists, responsible for negotiations with employers (mostly state and municipal). At the same time, its main concern is the science of psychology. It publishes jointly with the other Scandinavian countries one journal in the Scandinavian languages and one in English. It publishes alone a biweekly journal for members, with a mixture of professional affairs and scientific papers; it publishes jointly with the organization of the school psychologists books and tests in the area of psychology.

The association is organized together with the other professional associations in Denmark (e.g., law, medicine, humanities, engineering) to negotiate wages and working conditions with the state and municipalities.

The association holds annual meetings and several conferences and courses on psychological items. In addition, it is a member of SAK (Scandinavian Psychological Associations: Sweden, Norway, Finland, and Iceland) and jointly holds a Scandinavian conference every 3 years.

Education and Training

Psychology is offered in three schools: the universities of Copenhagen and Aarhus, and the Royal Danish College of Education (only for teachers). Psychological degrees are state-controlled: candidate of psychology (6–7 years study), magister artium (6–7 years study), candidate of pedagogical psychology (3–4 years study to serve as school psychologists). The highest degree is doctor of philosophy. Approximately 3,500 students study psychology.

Governmental Supervisory System

The government exercises control over programs and number and quality of teachers (professors, associate professors, and assistant professors), as well as exams by external examiners. The state pays all salaries; the tuition is free.

Legal Status

A law for psychologists is under preparation or consideration. Only fully examined psychologists can work as psychologists in public positions, which constitute 95% of the positions for psychologists in Denmark at the moment. Anyone can start a private practice, but only a very few do; the title of psychologist is not protected by law. Professional ethics apply only to members (76% of the psychologists in Denmark belong to the psychological association.)

Research

Most research in Denmark within the area of psychology is funded by the National Science Foundation. Some research facilities and funds are also available at the universities and the Royal College of Education. There are also research facilities in the Danish National Social Science Institute and in the Danish Institutes of Educational Research.

Publications

Dansk Psykolognyt, Sct. Pedersstraede 34–36, 1453 København K; twice a month.

Nordisk Psykologi (in Scandinavian languages, published by Scandinavian Psychological Association), Akademisk Forlag, St. Kanikkestraede 8, 1169 København K; four times a year.

Scandinavian Journal of Psychology (in English, published as above), Almqvist and Wiksell Periodical Company, P. O. Box 62, 2-101 20 Stockholm, Sweden.

Skolepsykologi, published by Association of School Psychologists, Kingosvej 64A, 3000 Helsingør; six times a year.

Denmark publishes about 100 scholarly books on psychology annually.

Opportunities for Foreign Psychologists

Opportunities are rather limited. Knowledge of the Danish language is required, although several foreign texts are widely used in Danish universities. Inquiries should be addressed to the Danish Psychological Association:

> Dansk Psykologforening
> Sct. Pederstraede 34–36
> DK 1453 København K
> Denmark

Ecuador[1]

National Organization

Ecuadorian psychologists belong to the Ecuadorian Society of Vocational Counselors. The address of the organization is:

Sociedad Ecuatoriana de Orientadores
Vocacionales (SEOV)
García Avilés 513 y Luque
Edificio Alprecht, P. O. Box 3934
Guayaquil, Ecuador

The official language of the sociedad is Spanish.

Internal Structure

The executive body of the SEOV is called directorio central (central board of directors) and is elected by an assembly of provincial delegates and representatives of the universities that have psychology departments.

Membership

The SEOV has 200 active members and 20 associate members.

Major Activities

The SEOV holds a national congress every 2 years and publishes yearbooks and a bimonthly newsletter.

[1]Based on information supplied by Rodolfo Panay Claros, president of the Sociedad Ecuatoriana de Orientadores Vocacionales, in Ecuador, and other sources.

Education and Training

In Ecuador there are 10 institutions in which students can study psychology as a profession. In Quito there is the Central University, where the psychology school grants the following titles or diplomas: psychologist, doctor in specialized psychology, psychology teacher, vocational counselor, licenciado in educational science with psychology specialization, and doctor in educational psychology. The Pontifical Catholic University with its psychology school grants the same titles. In Guayaquil, the University of Guayaquil grants the titles of psychology teacher, vocational counselor, and licenciado in psychology. The Catholic University Santiago de Guayaquil grants the title of specialized psychologist, which is in clinical psychology. Psychology students in pedagogy obtain the titles of psychology pedagogues as teachers, licenciados, and doctors. In the University Laica Vicente Rocafuerte of Guayaquil, the titles of psychology pedagogue as teachers, licenciados, and doctors are given. In Manabí, there is a branch of this last university giving the same titles. In Esmeraldas, the Technical University of Esmeraldas grants the same type of titles in educational psychology that are given by the Catholic University Santiago de Guayaquil. In Loja, its university grants the titles of psychology teacher of secondary schools, vocational counselor, licenciado in psychology. The Cuenca University in Cuenca grants the title of psychology teacher.

Legal Status

The Ecuadorian universities send to the Ministry of Education four lists of their students who have received an academic degree. This procedure legalizes the degree and the titles.

Publications

The following magazines are related to psychology: *DOP Archivos Ecuatorianos de Orientación* of the University of Quito; *Archivos de Criminología, Neurosiquiatría, y Disciplinas Conexas,* issued by the publication department of the University of Guayaquil; *Anales de Psicología,* issued by the publication department of the University of Guayaquil; *Psychology School Magazine* and *Magazine of the Psychology School Association,* issued by the same department of the University of Guayaquil.

Occupational Distribution

Ecuadorian psychologists teach in universities and high schools, mostly as vocational counselors.

Opportunities for Foreign Psychologists

Ecuadorian universities welcome foreigners as visiting professors. Foreign psychologists interested in permanent employment must have their degrees approved by the University of Guayaquil in Guayaquil, Ecuador.

Egypt[1]

National Organization

The national psychological organization of the Arab Republic of Egypt is the

Egyptian Society for Psychological Studies
Tager Building
1 Osiris Street
Garden City, Cairo, Egypt
The official language is Arabic.

Internal Structure

The society is run by a council, which consists of nine members elected at the annual general meeting. Among the functions of the council are to prepare the internal rules and regulations, to form the committees necessary to fulfill the aims of the society, to call ordinary and/or extraordinary meetings according to rules, and to put into effect the resolutions of the general meeting. The council is elected by secret ballot at the annual general meeting for 3 years. Election of one-third of the members of the council is held every year.

Membership

The total number of members of the society is about 120. There are three categories of membership: *Members* must be

---

[1]Based on information supplied by Alexandria University in Egypt and submitted by Ahmed M. Azzam, director of the Cultural and Educational Bureau of the Embassy of the Arab Republic of Egypt in Washington, D.C., and other sources.

psychology graduates, able to contribute to the actualization of the objectives and resolutions of the society; *fellows* must be members of the society for at least 7 years and must have made outstanding scientific contributions to psychology or have rendered outstanding services to psychology; *affiliated members* must have a university degree and should be interested in psychological studies and be willing to benefit from the activities of the society.

Major Activities

The major activities of the society are lectures and/or symposia held at least once a month on topics related to psychology, and scientific conferences held every 3 or 4 years.

Education and Training

Four Egyptian universities offer training in psychology. They are: Cairo University, Faculty of Arts, Psychology Department; Ein-Shams University, Faculty of Arts, Psychology Department, Girls College, Psychology Department, Faculty of Education, Department of Educational Psychology; Alexandria University, Faculty of Arts, Psychology Department, Faculty of Education, Department of Educational Psychology; El-Azhar University, Girls College, Psychology Department, Faculty of Education, Department of Educational Psychology. Advanced studies and degrees are offered by Cairo University (postgraduate diploma of applied psychology) and the Ein-Shams University Faculty of Arts (postgraduate diploma of psychological services.

Legal Status

A bachelor of arts in psychology is considered enough qualification by all government departments for the applicant to work as a psychologist. The Ministry of Public Health, however, encourages psychologists (after being appointed) to obtain the postgraduate diploma of Cairo University, as this diploma is very much slanted toward clinical psychology.

A psychologist who wishes to have private practice has to be licensed by the Ministry of Health. The law governing private practice was passed in 1956, but is being reviewed at the moment by the National Assembly.

Research

Psychology departments of the Egyptian universities give some financial support to research projects carried out by members of the staff. The National Center for Social and Criminological Research, Cairo, provides a large number of research facilities.

Publications

The National Review of Social Sciences is a quarterly, published by the National Center for Social and Criminological Research.

The National Review of Criminological Science is a quarterly, published by the National Center for Social and Criminological Research.

A journal for lay readers is published bimonthly by the Egyptian Society for Mental Health under the caption *Journal of Mental Health.*

Opportunities for Foreign Psychologists

Foreign psychologists are invited for limited periods as experts or visiting professors. For detailed information, one must contact Egyptian consular services.

Fiji[1]

Education and Training

All Fiji psychologists are foreign-trained. The University of the South Pacific at Laucala Bay, Suva, Fiji, operates a psychological assessment unit jointly with the Fiji government. The task of the unit is research and service in developing mental tests.

Opportunities for Foreign Psychologists

Foreign psychologists interested in employment should contact the School of Education of the above university, or Fiji consular services.

[1]Based on information supplied by Dr. N. Sbhandoa, School of Education, the University of the South Pacific.

Finland[1]

National Organizations

Finland has two psychological organizations. The national organization to which most psychologists belong is the

Finnish Psychological Society
Building of Scientific Societies
Smellmanink 9-11
0170 Helsinki 17
Finland

The Finnish Association of Psychologists deals with professional matters, especially with psychologists employed in industry, clinical positions, vocational guidance, and education. The address of this association is the

Finnish Association of Psychologists
Vocational Guidance Bureau
Siltasaarenk 16A
Helsinki
Finland

The official language in both organizations is Finnish.

Membership Requirements

Members are admitted to both organizations on the basis of a university degree.

---

[1]Based on information supplied by various sources.

Education and Training

The universities of Helsinki, Turku, Jyväskylä, and Tampere, as well as the Institute of Technology in Otaniemi offer full training programs for psychologists. Each university stresses certain aspects and areas; e.g., the Helsinki University offers training in clinical, developmental, and educational psychology, and the Turku University specializes in experimental, comparative, and developmental psychology.

All Finnish universities offer a variety of courses on undergraduate levels. At least 2 more years of study are required for the master's degree, and another 2 years for the licentiate title. Doctor's degrees are awarded on the basis of a scholarly dissertation.

Legal Status

The Ministry of Education supervises and approves university degrees and cooperates with the organizations of Finnish psychologists.

Research

Most psychological research is conducted at the universities. The Helsinki University specializes in perception, clinical and developmental, social, and educational psychology. The Turku University conducts experimental research in learning, perception, developmental, and comparative fields. The research at the Tampere University is mainly related to personality and social issues. The Jyväskylä University engages in developmental and educational psychology as well as testing and measurements.

The Institute of Technology at Otaniemi has a special Institute of Industrial Psychology, and its research work encompasses several areas of personnel, organizational, and other aspects of industrial psychology.

The Finnish government supports applied research

through its Vocational Guidance Bureau, Institute of Occupational Health, and other agencies.

Publications

Finnish psychologists participate in the Scandinavian journal, *Nordisk Psykologi.*

Opportunities for Foreign Psychologists

Finnish universities welcome foreign experts for short-term lectureships, research, and other temporary assignments. Foreign psychologists should address their inquiries to Finnish consulates, or directly to one of the universities.

France[1]

Introduction

Psychology in France has a long and glorious tradition, starting with French philosophy through the encyclopedists to contemporary psychology. French scholars and scientists have made significant contributions to neuropsychology (Flourens), to physiological and experimental psychology (Pieron, Dumas), to social psychology (E. Durckheim, Levy-Bruhl), to dynamic psychology (Maine de Biran), to hypnotism (Bernheim, Charcot), to genetics (Ribot), to the study of the unconscious (Pierre Janet), and to intelligence tests (Alfred Binet).

At the present time, scores of French psychologists actively pursue research in diversified fields, such as perception (P. Fraisse, R. Frances, G. Noizet, and others), learning and memory (P. Fraisse, M. Denis, C. George, and others), psycholinguistics (J. Segui, G. Noizet, and others), psychology of individual differences (M. Bruchon, F. Longest, and others), developmental psychology (P. Oleron, B. Zazzo), abnormal psychology (P. Oleron, R. Perron, and B. Zazzo), and social psychology (R. Frances, Y. Bernard, and M. Percheux).

National Organization

The national society of French psychologists is the
Société Française de Psychologie (SFP)
28, rue Serpente
75 006 Paris, France
The official language is French.

[1]Based on information supplied by Robert Pages, general secretary of the Société Française de Psychologie, and other sources.

Internal Structure

The business of the SFP is conducted by the executive bureau. The bureau exécutif includes president, vice-president, secretary general, and treasurer. Together with representatives of specialized sections and regional associations, it constitutes the national bureau. The members of the bureau exécutif are nominated by the bureau fédéral and elected by the annual assemblée générale.

Membership

The SFP has about 1,500 regular and associate members. The SFP has seven divisions (sections): (1) Section de Psychologie Clinique, (2) Section de Psychologie de l'Enfant et de l'Education, (3) Section de Psychologie Expérimentale, (4) Section de Psychophysiologie, (5) Section de Psychologie Sociale, (6) Section de Psychologie du Travail, and (7) Section Enseignement.

Membership Requirements

The minimum admission requirement for membership is the degree of maîtrise de psychologie or its equivalent.

Major Activities

The SFP organizes national scientific meetings once a year in May, held in Paris or in the provinces. Other conferences are organized by regional initiative or a specialized section or any combinations. The SFP conducts training seminars and publishes the monthly, *Bulletin de Psychologie*.

Education and Training

Almost all French universities in Paris and in the provinces as well as a few private schools offer psychological training. They grant the diplomas of licence, maîtrise, and doctorat. The number of students varies from thousands on the lower levels to 15 or a few score in post-maîtrise (doctoral) programs. The grades and professorships and generally the teaching positions are controlled by government or at least supervised through responsible elections by universities, the names being taken from lists of aptitude established by the National Advisory Committee.

Most problems of education in psychology are discussed within the SFP (mostly in its special section on teaching) by the SFP members who are in charge of all levels of teaching responsibilities.

Legal Status

The SFP has established an ethical code. It is very influential in the profession but with no formal disciplinary procedures except for membership problems.

Research

Highly diversified research in several fields of psychology is conducted by the Centre National de la Recherche Scientifique (CNRS), which employs several professional workers, at all levels, and technical research assistants (either psychologists or others). Most laboratory research is connected or integrated with research organizations of the various universities.

Financial support for research is offered by a few other governmental agencies (Institut National de la Santé et de la Recherche Médicale) and agencies linked with other government departments. Universities manage their own funds, which are frequently pooled with those from research agencies proper, such as the Centre National de la Recherche Scientifique.

Publications

French psychologists publish several scientific journals, as follows:

Année Psychologique, published with the support of the CNRS, 28, Rue Serpente, 75 006 Paris. The *Année* is published twice a year.

Bulletin de Psychologie, 17 rue de la Sorbonne, 75 005 Paris, published monthly by the SFP.

Bulletin du Centre d'Etudes et de Recherche Psychotechniques (CERP), published under the auspices of the CNRS. Its address is 13 place de Villiers, 93 Montreuil.

Bulletin Signalétique du CNRS—Section 390—Psychologie et psychopathologie, psychiatrie, published by the CNRS. The address is 26 rue Boyer, Paris cedex 20.

Journal de Psychologie Normale et Pathologique, published with the support of the CNRS at 9 Rue Edouard Détaille, 92 100 Boulogne Billancourt, a quarterly.

Revue de Psychologie Appliquée, 48 avenue Victor Hugo, 75 783 Paris cedex 16, a quarterly.

Travail Humain, published with the support of the CNRS, 41 rue Guy Lussac, 75 005 Paris, appears twice a year.

Cognition—*International Journal of Cognitive Psychology,* The Hague, Paris, Mouton, is a quarterly.

The main handbooks recently published are:

P. Fraisse et J. Piaget, *Traité de Psychologie Expérimentale,* nine volumes, Presses Universitaires de France (PUF).

M. Reuchlin (dir.), *Traité de Psychologie Appliquée,* ten volumes (PUF).

A. Gratiot-Alphandery et R. Zazzo (dirs.), *Traité de Psychologie de l'Enfant,* five volumes (PUF).

M. Debesse et G. Mialaret (dirs.), *Traité des Sciences Pedagogiques,* seven volumes (PUF).

Several collections of research books have been published:

Monographies Françaises de Psychologie, CNRS, 15 quai A. France 75 007 Paris.

Collection SUP, Section La Psychologie, dirigée par Paul Fraisse.

Collection Psychologie d'Aujourd'hui, dirigée par Paul Fraisse (PUF).

Collection Bibliothèque Scientifique Internationale, section Psychologie, dirigée par Paul Fraisse (PUF). *Collection Bibliothèque de Psychanalyse* (PUF), dirigée par Jean Laplanche.

The *Vocabulaire de la Psychologie,* compiled by the late Henri Pieron, is frequently revised.

A directory of work by psychologists has been edited and a general directory of psychologists is in preparation.

Occupational Distribution

French psychologists work in a variety of fields. Most of them are involved in university teaching and research, but many work in schools as school psychologists and guidance counselors, and increasing numbers turn to industrial and clinical psychology.

Opportunities for Foreign Psychologists

Foreign experts are welcome in France, especially if they are interested in research. The arrangements are usually on a 1-year basis but they can be renewed. Applicants should address themselves to a particular university or research center.

Germany[1]

Introduction

Toward the end of the 19th century and in the first three decades of the 20th century, Germany was the greatest single center of psychological research and thought. In 1879 Wilhelm Wundt established in Leipzig the first psychological laboratory. The experimental studies were conducted in several academic centers by a growing number of psychologists, among them Ebbinghaus, Külpe, Neumann, and Ach. Several schools in psychology have their roots in Germany, among them structuralism, phenomenology, Gestalt, and personalistic and humanistic psychology.

The Nazi regime put an end to the flourishing psychological science. A great many prominent German psychologists emigrated to foreign countries, and some who did not escape were put in concentration camps.

After World War II Germany was divided in two. The smaller eastern part formed the German Democratic Republic and the larger part in the west was established as the Federal German Republic.

German Democratic Republic

National Organization

About two-thirds of the 600 psychologists in East Germany belong to the psychological society. Its address is

[1]Based on information supplied by various sources.

Gesellschaft für Psychologie der Deutschen
Demokratischen Republik
Am Kupfergraben 7
108 Berlin
German Democratic Republic

Divisions

The psychological society has four divisions, namely, clinical, educational, social, and industrial.

Education and Training

There are 37 universities. Twenty offer psychology courses and 12 offer advanced training in various areas of psychology. University degrees are granted on two levels, namely, diploma (diplom psychologe) and doctorate. Candidates for the diploma must write a thesis and pass a staff examination in psychological theory in a field of the student's specialization, dialectic materialism, and elements of neurology and psychiatry.

Research

The universities that offer advanced training also engage in psychological research. The Karl Marx University in Leipzig conducts research in developmental and educational psychology. The Humboldt University in Berlin engages in research in clinical, industrial, and physiological psychology. The technical university in Dresden conducts research in industrial psychology. The German Academy of Sienna, Department of Clinical Psychology, is involved in studies in neuropathology and treatment of mental disorders.

Publications

The *Zeitschrift für Psychologie* is published annually.

Occupational Distribution

Most psychologists in the German Democratic Republic are engaged in teaching and research, especially along Pavlovian lines.

Opportunities for Foreign Psychologists

Foreign psychologists who wish to visit research centers and universities in the German Democratic Republic and/or conduct research there must write to the
Staatssekretariat für das Hoch und Fachschulwesen
Otto Grotewohl Strasse 64
108 Berlin 8
German Democratic Republic

German Federal Republic

National Organizations

There are 10,000 psychologists in West Germany and most of them are members of the psychological society called the
Deutsche Gesellschaft für Psychologie
Psychologisches Institut der Universität Hamburg
Von Mellepart 6
D-2000 Hamburg 13
German Federal Republic
About 3,500 applied psychologists, among them clinical, industrial, and school psychologists, belong to the
Berufsverband Deutscher Psychologen
Oskar-Sommer Strasse 20
Frankfurt a. Main
German Federal Republic

Major Activities

Every other year the psychological society holds a scientific congress. The retiring president of the society presents to the congress a biannual report on the state of the society and on the development of psychology as a science and an occupation.

Education and Training

Forty-two universities in the German Federal Republic and West Berlin train psychologists. The number of faculty members who teach psychology is 667, the number of students majoring in psychology is 13,000, and at present there are 740 Ph.D. candidates in the German Federal Republic (the Bundesrepublik).

On February 2, 1973, the Bundesrepublik instituted a formal examination for a diploma in psychology. The examination is composed of two parts, the pretest and the test itself. Those who pass both parts are called diplom-psychologe, or dipl. psych., which corresponds to certified psychologist in the United States.

The pretest is conducted in the following areas: (1) methodology, (2) general psychology I, (3) general psychology II, (4) developmental psychology, (5) psychology of individual differences and personality studies, (6) social psychology, and (7) physiological psychology or physiological issues relevant to psychological studies.

Every university decides in which area preexamination will be given, and whether it will be written, oral, or both. The local universities also determine the timetable of the preexaminations.

Those who pass the pretest are eligible for the diploma test itself. This test is directed to three major areas: (1) methods (diagnostics and other methods and techniques), (2) applied psychology, and (3) basic science.

Research

Psychological research is mainly conducted in the universities. In 1978 the German Research Society *(Deutsche Forschungs Gemeinschaft)* reported the following research work: (1) development of mathematical models (for instance,

in learning, memory, and testing); (2) education; (3) behavior modification; (4) social perception; (5) biofeedback and its therapeutic application; and (6) psycholinguistics.
Thought processes, neuropsychology, physiological psychology, and perception are also studied.
The Max Planck Institute engages in physiological psychology. The University of Bonn conducts research in personality, developmental psychology, cognitive process, and motivation. The University of Heidelberg conducts research in clinical, developmental, and experimental psychology. The Free University of Berlin and the University of Frankfurt a. Main engage in diversified research activities.

Publications

The psychological society publishes the journal *Psychologische Rundschau.*

Occupational Distribution

There are in Germany about 10,000 psychologists earning a living in their profession, and about 15,000 students aspiring to the psychological diploma. The majority of German psychologists is involved in teaching and research, about one-third of all German psychologists are clinicians, and about one-eighth are working in industrial counseling and school psychology. Applied psychologists have their own organization, *Berufsverband Deutscher Psychologen.*

Opportunities for Foreign Psychologists

West German universities and research centers welcome foreign psychologists as visiting professors and researchers. For information, one should write to
Deutscher Akademischer Austausch Dienst
Frankengraben 50
532 Bad Godesberg
German Federal Republic

Greece[1]

National Organization

The national psychological organization is the
Greek Psychological Society
13 Amerikis Street
Athens, Greece
The official language is Greek.

Internal Structure

The business of the society is conducted by a seven-member executive committee consisting of the president, the vice-president, the secretary, the treasurer, and three committee members. The executive committee organizes scientific and professional activities and forms ad hoc committees that deal with various problems of the society. At present, there are a number of such committees trying to define the types of services that psychologists could offer to the community, and the kind of training required from psychologists.

The executive committee is elected every 2 years in a general meeting by the regular members of the society.

Membership

The total membership of the Greek Psychological Society is 88. The members of the society belong to one of the follow-

[1]Based on information supplied by Prof. Lambros Houssiadas, University of Thessaloniki, Greece, and other sources.

ing three categories: (1) regular members, (2) temporary members (i.e., members not yet accorded full status), and (3) honorary members.

Membership Requirements

Psychologists are accepted as regular members by the society after they have practiced for at least 1 year. They should be in possession of one of the following: (1) a Ph.D. degree from an established (accredited) foreign university, or a Ph.D. degree in psychology from a Greek university; (2) an M.A. or "license" degree; (3) a B.A. degree from a philosophy school of a Greek university, plus 2 years of postgraduate study in psychology at a foreign university.

Psychologists are accepted as temporary members if they have any of the qualifications mentioned above but have not yet practiced their profession for at least a year.

The status of honorary members is bestowed by the society by a unanimous vote of the executive committee; this status is accorded to scientists from Greece or from other countries who have contributed to the promotion of psychology as either a basic or an applied science.

Education and Training

Training in psychology is offered by the Psychology and Education Section of the School of Philosophy of the Aristotelian University of Thessaloniki. A less extensive course in psychology is offered by the School of Philosophy of the University of Ioannina, a relatively new university (established in 1964) in the northwest of Greece. In addition, a number of private institutes are offering courses in psychology.

B.A. degrees with a major in psychology are offered by the School of Philosophy of the University of Thessaloniki. The same school offers the postgraduate diploma in psychology. Students for this diploma are required to take a 2-year course in psychology and two ancillary subjects of their choice (e.g., education and philosophy). At the end of their 2-year course they are required to submit a thesis.

Opportunities for Foreign Psychologists

There are not many openings for psychologists in Greece at present. Inquiries should be directed to the

Ministry of Coordination
5 Hippokratos Street
Athens, Greece

Hong Kong[1]

Introduction

While the formal establishment of an independent department of psychology was not achieved until 1967, there were a number of earlier developments in Hong Kong that were of great importance. These included the establishment of government psychiatric services in 1948.

There has been an urgent requirement for expert services in child guidance. These have been provided by the government's Special Education Section, which includes educational psychologists as well as audiometricians, speech experts, etc. Child guidance services were also provided by Hong Kong University, as well as by churches.

While the teaching in psychology began at the University of Hong Kong in 1948, the first department of psychology was founded in 1967.

Hong Kong Psychological Society (HKPsS)

The Hong Kong Psychological Society was established in 1968 to develop psychology in Hong Kong in a wider context. The aims of the society are to encourage the growth of psychology in Hong Kong and the development of an appropriate professional environment. The society has the following categories of professional membership: honorary fellows, fellows, associate members, graduate members, foreign affiliates, and visiting members. The nonprofessional members include

[1]Based on information supplied by John L. M. Binnie Dawson, University of Hong Kong.

subscriber members and student subscribers. The society is further concerned with the establishment of professional standards and offering advisory services to government and other organizations concerning the professional role and standards of psychologists.

The society draws its membership from the Hong Kong and Chinese universities and from government and private organizations. In 1972 the society was admitted to the International Union of Scientific Psychology, which ensures that members have worldwide professional recognition and can attend international congresses.

International Association for Cross-Cultural Psychology (IACCP)

The IACCP was founded in Hong Kong in 1972 and had its first international conference at the University of Hong Kong in the same year. The second international conference was held in Canada in 1974 and the third in Holland in 1976. The aims of the society are to facilitate communication between cross-cultural psychologists, to further the advancement of research and methodology in cross-cultural psychology, and to more effectively test the universal validity of psychological theories in branches of psychology. These aims are achieved by holding IACCP national, regional, and international conferences. Further, the IACCP publishes the *Journal of Cross-Cultural Psychology,* the *IACCP Newsletter,* and complete conference proceedings.

Education and Training

The University of Hong Kong

Department of Psychology. This department was founded by Professor Dawson in 1976. It was separated from the combined philosophy/psychology department. The department, although based in the faculty of social sciences, also teaches in the arts, science, and medical faculties.

The University of Hong Kong follows the British honors degree system with a 2-year sixth form followed by a 3-year honors degree. Teaching involves seminars, tutorials, lectures, and experiments, as well as research theses. Where the content of the undergraduate degrees comprises certain required compulsory courses and at least 50% of the total degree, these degrees are recognized by the British Psychological Society. Psychology I is a prerequisite for the 2nd and 3rd years. The undergraduate combinations are set out below.

Undergraduate Psychology Combinations. The eight-course combination involves a selection of only psychology papers during the final 2 years.

The four-plus-four combinations in the social sciences consist of psychology plus economics, psychology plus sociology, psychology plus industrial studies, psychology plus statistics, psychology plus political science, psychology plus management studies, psychology plus social work.

Arts. The courses involved are psychology plus English and psychology plus philosophy.

The six-plus-two combinations in the social sciences consist of psychology plus philosophy, psychology plus statistics, psychology plus economics, psychology plus political science, psychology plus social work, psychology plus management, psychology plus sociology.

Medical Faculty. An introductory course in psychology related to medicine is taught to medical students in their 2nd year.

Science Faculty. A course in neuroanatomy is taught in collaboration with other departments. Psychology I, physiological psychology, and animal behavior are also to be introduced.

The Chinese University of Hong Kong

The Hong Kong University is related to the Anglo-Chinese school system, with a 2-year sixth form, with teaching in English and an entrance exam in English; the Chinese University is tied to the Chinese secondary system, where the teaching is in Chinese. There is only 1 year in the sixth form followed by a 4-year degree, which is structurally very similar to the United States degree, although honors classifications are awarded.

The Department of Sociology (CUHK) Subdepartment of Psychology. The psychology program offered at the Chinese University is only a minor at this time, but it is planned to develop as a major at a later date.

The Baptist College

This is a 4-year college that also has an American structure and offers extensive teaching in psychology.

The Hong Kong Polytechnic

This is Hong Kong's technological university; it offers psychology-related courses in certain departments and there is also a counseling service for the students.

Research

The University of Hong Kong—Department of Psychology. The department has excellent laboratory facilities for psychological research and teaching supported by technicians, laboratory attendants, animal technicians, and workshops. There is a 1st-year laboratory, a 2nd/3rd-year laboratory, a perception laboratory, a biosocial laboratory, an ergonomics laboratory, an acoustics laboratory, a physiological psychology laboratory, an animal behavior laboratory, animal holding rooms, a developmental clinical laboratory with multiracial playground, and a PDP8 on-line control computer system. The range of equipment for these laboratories also covers most branches of psychology.

The multilingual context of Hong Kong has stimulated many research programs aimed at understanding these issues, among them bilingual semantic merging and acculturation in Hong Kong. Eye movements in the perception of Chinese characters were studied in terms of information theory. Contingent variation (CNV) of Hong Kong schizophrenics and normals were among the research topics.

The biosocial conceptual system was developed to study the relationships between the biological environment social organization and the development of adaptive psychological skills that have survival value.

The different biosocial effects of Temne and Mende agricultural ecosystems in West Africa have been reported by Dawson (1969, 1975, 1978). The effects of Temne and Eskimo differences in biosocial adaptation have also been studied in terms of socialization, resulting in significant differences in cognitive style reported in research papers.

An experimental program using rats has confirmed the effects of opposite sex hormones in adults and neonates in reversing sex-associated spatial and activity skills.

A biosocial laterality model has been postulated to explain the distribution of handedness in a society, in terms of cultural pressures toward conformity; these are held to interact with a genetic model to determine the incidence of left-handedness in a society.

Kao has carried out a series of studies in ergonomics dealing with the effects of intermittency on feedback on a compensatory tracking task, while he has also studied user preference toward handwriting instruments.

Several studies have dealt with the personality structure of Chinese with particular reference to the processes of filial piety, dogmatism, and creativity.

The University of Hong Kong—School of Education. Research programs are carried out in many areas, including educational psychology and psychometrics.

The University of Hong Kong—Center of Asian Studies. This center accepts visiting fellows who may be interested in carrying out psychological research.

The Chinese University—Institute for Social Sciences. This institute has organized and published extensive research projects relating to sociological, psychological, and social-work problems at varying occupational and socioeconomic levels of Hong Kong society.

Research, Testing, and Guidance Center—Hong Kong Government. This center is part of the Hong Kong government education department and deals mainly with research and construction of psychological attainment tests that are administered to school populations as required. While the Special Education Section of the Hong Kong government is more concerned with guidance and counseling programs, they carry out research programs as well.

Mental Health Association of Hong Kong. The Mental Health Association has organized extensive research programs in Hong Kong, as well as publishing a recent book describing the current state of mental health activities in Hong Kong.

Clinical Practice

The graduate program in clinical psychology, leading to the H.K.U. M.Soc.Sci. degree has been in active operation since 1971 with a biennial intake limited to six students. The original limitation on the number of students was due to questions concerning job opportunities for placement in appropriate agencies during the training period.

During the past 5 years the British Psychological Society has investigated the graduate program in clinical psychology and has recognized the program as acceptable, granting to H.K.U. graduates all rights and privileges that similarly trained clinical psychologists enjoy in the United Kingdom.

In addition, various social welfare and voluntary agencies have vacancies and are engaged in the search for qualified clinical psychologists. Clinical placements during the training period have proven to be available and constructive, and include:

Castle Peak Hospital   Caritas Centre
Hong Kong Psychiatric Center   Yang Center
Special Education Division   Lutheran World Center
(Education Department)
United Christian Hospital   H.K.U. Counselling Center

Industrial Practice

There are very few trained industrial psychologists in Hong Kong, but this should be overcome when the new degree is introduced. There is already a Hong Kong University undergraduate program in industrial studies and psychology that will possibly help.

There are a number of market survey firms active in Hong Kong, as well as management consultants who have some trained industrial psychologists. The Hong Kong Productivity Center is also very oriented toward industrial psychology and even runs occasional courses for personnel officers in psychological measurement and testing.

Legal Status

There is no legal registration required in Hong Kong for professional psychologists. However, the Hong Kong Psychological Society has certain prerequisites before undergraduate and graduate degrees in psychology can be recognized. Furthermore, the graduate memberships, associateships, and fellowships of this society require certain levels of academic qualifications and professional experience before recognition can be granted.

Opportunities for Foreign Psychologists

There are opportunities for foreign psychologists to work in the University of Hong Kong, the Chinese University of Hong Kong, and the Baptist College, in government and commercial institutions, and in private practice. There may, however, be some language problems in certain areas such as clinical psychology and counseling, but it is possible for foreign psychologists to work in these areas once they gain some basic understanding of the language and culture of the Chinese people with whom they have to work.

Psychologists wishing to work in Hong Kong should have qualifications such that they would be recognized professionally by the Hong Kong Psychological Society for the particular field in which they propose to practice.

Hungary[1]

National Organization

All psychologists in the Hungarian People's Republic belong to the Hungarian Psychological Scientific Association. The official name of the society is

Magyar Pszichologiai Társaság
Hungarian Psychological Scientific Association
H-1124 Budapest XII, Meredek U. 1.
Hungary

The official language of the society is Hungarian.

Internal Structure

The society has an executive committee of 35 members, a presidium of 9 members, a president, a general secretary, and two deputy-general secretaries.

Between two assemblies, the presidium directs the activities of the society, regularly calling meetings of the larger plenum (the executive committee), reporting to the executive committee, and asking its advice.

The society has 12 chairmen of sections, who are ex-officio members of the executive committee, and each section has a presidium of its own comprising three to five people. The society has an ethical committee under the supervision of the executive committee and a three-member accounting com-

[1]Based on information supplied by the Hungarian Psychological Scientific Association, and other sources.

mittee, responsible for the basic direction of the society between two sessions of the general assembly. The general secretary is responsible for coordination of the work of sessions, with the help of his two deputies, who are responsible for different branches of psychology. He also deals with international relations. Both the president and the general secretary report to the presidium and finally to the assembly.

The general assembly is called together every 5 years. It elects the president and the general secretary, plus the members of the executive committee. The executive committee in turn elects the deputy-general secretaries and the members of the presidium.

Membership

The total number of members is about 800. Founding members number about 111, and regular members close to 700. There are 4 supporting legal members.

In 1978, the membership in the various sections was as follows: general psychology—50, social psychology—60, educational psychology—162, work group on child pathology —50, psychology of special education—50, criminal psychology—25, military psychology—35, sport psychology—50, psychology of traffic—35, industrial psychology—50, working group on vocational guidance—30.

Membership Requirements

Founding members are the members who founded the society in 1963. Regular members are recommended by two members of the section in which they wish to work, and then their admittance is approved by the general assembly. Supporting legal members help the society financially. Honorary members are elected by the assembly for their scientific merits. A university degree is a prerequisite for being admitted to regular membership.

Major Activities

The aims of the society are the cultivation and development of different branches of psychological sciences in Hungary and the promotion of the practical applications of this science. The association holds a general scientific congress every 5 years. The various sections organize specific conferences in their respective fields of study. The sections also organize scientific lectures, roundtables, workshops, case-study meetings, etc.

Education and Training

Psychology is taught at all Hungarian universities and teachers' colleges. A full training program in psychology is offered at the Eotvos Leorand University in Budapest, especially in the fields of clinical, educational, and industrial psychology. The curriculum includes courses in scientific methods, statistics, learning theory, comparative psychology, and Marxist philosophy. The teachers' college in Pecs trains psychologists in educational and cognitive psychology.

The University of Medicine in Budapest offers courses and practicum in psychopathology and neuropathology and in diagnostic and therapeutic methods.

The Kossuth Lajos University in Debrecen emphasizes educational psychology. The Budapest College for Special Education trains teachers and clinicians in diagnostic and remedial methods.

A candidate may secure the following: (1) diploma of psychologist; (2) diploma of psychologist—specialist in the fields of educational, clinical, or industrial psychology; (3) Ph.D. in psychology; (4) candidate of psychological sciences; and (5) doctor of psychological sciences.

The first three types of degrees are given by the universities, the last two by the Hungarian Academy of Sciences, through its Committee of Scientific Qualification. The last two are the highest scientific degrees.

1. For the diploma of psychology, 25 to 45 students are enrolled every year in regular daytime courses (5 years of study), about 150 students in all. There are 20 to 40 students every year in night classes (6 years of study), over 100 students in all.

2. There is no special program for a Ph.D. One must submit a dissertation and take the exams if he has the necessary qualifications. Ph.D. degrees number about 15 annually.

3. As candidates of psychological sciences, two or three people enter the 3-year program, which is independent study and research under the guidance of an expert in the field selected for dissertation. The degree is awarded after the defense of the dissertation. One to three people every year are allowed by the committee to apply for the degree on the basis of their scientific merits, without the 3-year program. They only take the exams required and defend their dissertation.

4. There is no program for the doctor of psychological sciences. Researchers are awarded this degree on the basis of an important dissertation after its defense. In 1978 there were eight doctors of psychological sciences in Hungary.

The Hungarian Ministry of Education, after consulting with special boards of experts, decides which schools can teach psychology as a major subject and what the requirements are for the various degrees.

The degrees of candidate and doctor of psychological sciences are given and supervised by the Committee of Scientific Qualifications of the Hungarian Academy of Sciences.

The Hungarian Psychological Society has no formal influence on the educational system, but its leading members are always invited to participate in the work of those committees that give advice to the Ministry of Education about the training of psychologists.

Legal Status—Licensing and Certification Requirements

Diploma of Psychologist. After 5 years of training in the daytime courses or 6 years in the night courses, the students submit a dissertation roughly equivalent to an M.A. dissertation and take a state board examination.

Diploma of Psychologist-Specialist. This diploma is granted after 2 to 3 years of special training in a field and after passing an examination in this special field.

Ph.D. in Psychology. This diploma is granted on the basis of a dissertation that has to be accepted by two university professors, after which a doctoral examination must be taken.

Candidate of Psychological Sciences. There are three ways to obtain the degree: (1) After 3 years of aspiranture, with a state grant and a tutor, the submitted dissertation has to contain new results in a certain field. It is accepted after two opponents criticize it, and it must be defended in a public academic debate. A committee decides if the dissertation and its defense have met the requirements. The candidate has to take an examination in two foreign languages and examinations in his particular field and in philosophy. (2) Those who work in institutions offering good opportunities for independent research can have a 1-year grant of aspiranture with a tutor, provided they have already started the work on the dissertation. (3) In the case where the person submits an already finished dissertation, after the dissertation is reviewed by "preopponents," he has the right to take the exams and defend the dissertation in the above-mentioned way.

Doctor of Psychological Sciences. In order to obtain this degree, an important, very original dissertation has to be submitted and defended in a public debate, after it has been criticized by three opponents. Only those having the degree of candidate of psychological sciences may apply for this degree.

The Ministry of Labor now regulates which diploma or degree is required by psychologists for different kinds of jobs. In order to work as a psychologist, one must have at least one of the five degrees mentioned. In order to become a "leader," for example, to be the head of a laboratory of industrial psychology, one must obtain at least the degree of specialist.

Professional Ethical Code and Disciplinary Procedures

The Hungarian Psychological Society formed a special committee to present a proposal for an ethical code for psychologists that would best suit the circumstances in Hungary. A legal expert participated in this work, and the committee studied all the available foreign examples. After the proposal had been discussed at different professional meetings and after all members of the society had been asked for comments, it was accepted—together with the modification proposals—by the general assembly of the Hungarian Psychological Society in January 1975. A few months later, its full text was published in the *Hungarian Journal of Psychology— Magyar Pszichológiai Szemle.*

This ethical code defends the professional and scientific independence of the psychologist toward his employer, with special regard to those colleagues who work in the practical field. At the same time, it sets rigorous standards of professional behavior and confidentiality. It puts great emphasis on the correct use of test methods and on the enforcement of the recommendations of the International Test Commission. The ethical code uses only moral sanctions, but the efficiency of the ethical standards is also promoted by the statute that governs the qualification and employment requirements of psychologists.

Research

Government Agencies. The main research center is the Psychological Research Institute of the Hungarian Academy of Sciences, where basic research is conducted in general, comparative, social, personality, developmental, and educational psychology.

In addition, in the research centers of the various (educational, industrial, or health) government institutions, applied research is conducted with financial support from the responsible ministry.

Universities. University teachers are required to dedicate half of their working time to research. The responsible ministry provides limited financial support. Actually, the teaching and administrative loads make for more than half of the working time, and instrumentation and assistance facilities are less adequate than in the research institutes. Still, a fairly substantial amount of research on general, developmental, and pedagogical psychology is conducted in the university departments.

There are no private research centers in Hungary.

Publications

Journals. There is only one journal entirely devoted to psychology: *Magyar Pszichológiai Szemle—Hungarian Journal of Psychology,* one volume in a year, six copies in a volume. The address is:

> Hungarian Journal of Psychology
> H-1083, Budapest, Bokay, J.u. 54
> Hungary

Two other journals give about half of their space to psychology:

Annales Universitatis Scientiarum Budapestiensis de Rolando Eötvös Nominatae—Sectio Paedagogica et Psychologica, one volume in a year, one copy in a volume. English, French, German, and Russian are used in the articles. The address is:

> Department of Pedagogy, University of Budapest
> H-1052, Budapest, Pesti B. u. 1
> Hungary

Ergonomia, one volume in a year, four copies in a volume. The address is:

> KG-ISSZI-Ergonomia
> H-1394 Budapest, 62 Pf. 356
> Hungary

There are no special lay journals in psychology, but many articles on psychology appear in general popular science journals or magazines.

Books. Scholarly books for the profession are mainly, but not exclusively, published by the academic publishers, with about 6 to 15 books a year.

Reference books rarely appear in Hungarian, perhaps one every other year. Educational textbooks are published mostly by the publishing house of the Ministry of Education, about five a year, including reprints. In addition a few hundred copies of about 10 to 15 mimeographed lecture notes or other educational materials are published for the students.

Books for the general public are published for the most part by a publishing house of popular science—about 5 to 10 books a year, including translations of foreign works.

Occupational Distribution

Industrial psychology is the main occupational avenue of Hungarian psychologists, and close to 40% of psychologists are employed in industry. Clinical and educational psychology come next, followed by research and teaching. There is no private practice in psychology in Hungary.

Opportunities for Foreign Psychologists

Foreign-trained psychologists who wish to work in Hungary, like any other professionals, have to ask for "nationalization" of their diploma by one of the Hungarian universities that gives training in psychology. The universities decide on an individual basis. The departments of psychology analyze the records and diplomas of the individual and either accept his diploma without any further requirements or require the person to take some additional examinations. Persons having a nationalized diploma have the same job opportunities as those trained in Hungary, provided their language proficiency allows for professional practice.

Hungarian schools of higher learning and research centers welcome visitors. Foreign psychologists interested in lecturing and/or research should write to the Hungarian Academy of Science as follows:

Institute of Psychology
Hungarian Academy of Science
Szondy 83/85
Budapest 6, Hungary

or:

Institute of Child Psychology
Hungarian Academy of Science
Szondy 83/85
Budapest 6, Hungary

Iceland[1]

National Organization

In 1964 Icelandic psychologists formed the
Society of Psychologists in Iceland
c/o Mr. Andri Isaksson
Hjalla Braut 14
Kopavogur, Iceland

Educational Facilities

The University of Iceland in Reykjavik offers courses in general, developmental, educational, and clinical psychology.

Occupational Distribution

Icelandic psychologists work in educational, clinical, and industrial psychology.

Opportunities for Foreign Psychologists

Iceland welcomes foreign psychologists, especially research workers and experts in applied fields. Inquiries should be addressed to Iceland's consulates.

[1]Based on information supplied by various sources.

India[1]

Introduction

Psychology as an independent field of study was first begun in India in 1916 at the University of Calcutta. This was followed by the University of Mysore in 1924, the University of Panjab in 1927, the University of Banaras in 1934, the University of Madras in 1943, and the University of Patna in 1946. The applied psychology section of the University of Calcutta was the only department in the country that had facilities for research in mental testing, educational psychology, and industrial psychology in the prewar era. Since the independence of the country in 1947, facilities for teaching and research in psychology increased considerably. By 1967–1968 as many as 32 universities had separate departments of psychology offering facilities for teaching and research at postgraduate levels.

Table I (H. C. Ganguli, 1974) gives the number of students enrolled for M.A. and Ph.D. degrees in psychology and the number of faculty members during the years 1962–1967.

National Organizations

In addition to universities, there are a number of national organizations where research work in different fields of psychology is undertaken. The important institutions are (1) National Council for Educational Research and Training

[1]Based on information supplied by T. E. Shanmugam, president, Indian Psychological Association.

Table 1. Number of Students and Faculty Members in Psychology in Indian Universities (1962–1967)

	1962–1963	1963–1964	1964–1965	1965–1966	1966–1967
Students for master's degree	1,191	1,452	1,614	1,806	1,761
Students for Ph.D. in psychology	99	113	146	182	188
Faculty members in psychology in the university departments and university colleges only	Not known		213	223	226

(NCERT), Delhi; (2) Directorate of Psychological Research in the Defense Science Organization of the Ministry of Defense, New Delhi; (3) Indian Institute of Management, Indian Agricultural Research Institute, Delhi; (4) Indian Institute of Mass Communication, Delhi; (5) National Institute of Community Development, Hyderabad; (6) National Institute of Family Planning, Delhi; (7) National Institute of Health Administration and Education, Delhi; (8) All India Institute of Public Health and Hygiene, Delhi; (9) Sri Ram Center for the Study of Developing Societies, Delhi; and (10) A.N. Institute of Social Studies, Patna.

There are three professional organizations of psychologists in India. They are the Indian Psychological Association, started in 1926; the Indian Academy of Applied Psychology, started in 1960; and the Association of Clinical Psychologists, started in 1968.

There are other associations, such as the Madras Psychology Society; the Maharashtra Psychology Association, Bombay; the Bihar Psychological Association; the Gujarat Psychological Association; and the Karnataka Psychological Association. In addition to these, the Indian Science Congress Association, which meets annually in the 1st week of January, has a section on psychology and education where scientific papers are read and symposia are held.

Practice

Practice of psychology is negligible in India. It is confined to consultancy to industries in major cities. Training in clinical psychology started in the 1960s, and the Association of Clinical Psychologists has not laid down any strict rules for practicing clinical psychologists. The clinical psychologist's work in India, at present, is confined to assisting psychiatrists in their hospital work.

Legal Status

There is no legal status for psychologists and they receive a certificate only from the universities and institutes where they have completed their studies or training.

Research

The survey of research in psychology published in 1971 by the Indian Council of Social Science Research gives details regarding the trend of research in 10 areas. From this it may be seen that there was increased output of publications after 1960. This is due to the opening of departments of psychology in 10 universities between 1950 and 1960 and in 17 more since 1960.

The average number of papers published for the period between 1950 and 1969 was 150 per year and the total number of publications in all areas of psychology between 1920 and 1969 was 1,950. The average number of papers in the late 1970s was close to 200. The total of 1,950 publications has been classified according to major areas (see Table 2).

It may be seen from Table 2 that social psychology (16%), experimental psychology (14%), mental testing (13%), and general psychology (11%) are the important areas of publication, accounting for about 54% of the total publication. Next in importance are industrial (9%), educational (8%), abnormal (6%), clinical (6%), and personality (6%), accounting for about 35% of the total publication. Indian psychology (2%) and

Table 2. Publications According to Major Areas

Area	N	Percentage of Total	Rank
General	207	10.6	4
Experimental	268	13.7	2
Social	309	15.9	1
Personality	112	5.7	9
Clinical	116	6.0	8
Abnormal	124	6.4	7
Mental testing	254	13.0	3
Industrial	156	8.6	5
Vocational	55	2.8	10
Educational	147	7.5	6
Educational statistics	3	.2	18
Child	47	2.4	12
Aesthetics	7	.4	17
Criminal	30	1.5	14
Indian psychology	39	2.0	13
Physiological psychology	53	2.7	11
Statistics	13	.7	15
Parapsychology	10	.5	16

parapsychology (5%), which has been given so much publicity, have a negligible percentage.

A brief summary of the research done in different areas of psychology brings out the advancement of psychology in India.

Clinical Psychology. Calcutta University was first in training young people in psychoanalysis as a method of psychotherapy. The Indian Psychoanalytic Society, founded in 1962 by Prof. Girindra Sekhar Bose, started the Lumbini Park Mental Hospital in Calcutta in 1940. Since then it has been rendering services to the community. The major clinical centers that train psychologists and provide supervised practicum or uniform training facilities are (1) All India Institute of Mental Health, Bangalore, (2) Hospital for Mental Diseases, Kanke, Ranchi, and (3) Mental Hospital, Lumbini Park, Calcutta.

All India Institute of Mental Health has trained 114 clinical psychologists from the date of its inception. The Indian

Psychoanalytic Society has been publishing a journal, *Samiska,* which is devoted to publishing the analytic work done in the Mental Hospital in Calcutta and elsewhere. In the field of clinical psychology, attempts have been made to study the various psychopathologies, particularly their diagnostic problems of evaluation and therapeutic intervention. Research in these areas has largely concentrated on adaptation of techniques and instruments.

Two institutions in the country operate clinics for treatment cases in speech pathology, and train personnel in speech therapy. One is the All India Institute of Speech and Hearing in Mysore and the other is the Nair Hospital, Bombay.

Delinquency in general, and juvenile delinquency in particular attracted greater attention from the angle of research. A number of tests have been developed and a few studies on criminals and their personality characteristics, drug addiction, suicide, and alcoholism have been carried out. Research in rehabilitation has also been done.

Developmental Psychology. Studies in developmental orientation have started only recently. Research in this area is concerned mainly with development of intelligence, abilities, interests, attitudes, emotionality, personality, and adjustment.

Educational Psychology. The first college of education was established in Madras more than 100 years ago. Instruction in educational psychology began in India in colleges of education at the time of the establishment of the first training college. However, being an applied branch of psychology, it neither attained importance on its own merits by faculties of education nor received adequate recognition in the departments of psychology. Studies were reported on such topics as attitude and adjustment, testing, educational and career guidance, school learning, and teaching methods.

Experimental Psychology. This has been divided into nine sections, namely, psychophysics, sensory process, perception, attention, reaction time, work fatigue, physiology of behavior—including animal behavior, learning, memory, and thinking—problem solving, and psycholinguistics. It is of interest to note that out of the 288 studies referred to in the review, only 112 were done after 1950. At the present time there is a good deal of sophistication in the design of experiments.

Industrial Psychology. Vocational choice, guidance, selection and placement, training, testing and work analysis, performance and job satisfaction, management, and engineering psychology are the areas covered. Among these only two areas—namely, performance and job satisfaction, and management and organization—have the largest concentration of study.

Psychological research in industry has had an academic orientation rather than being viewed as a discipline that is likely to produce immediate and useful results capable of application in industry. This notion has retarded research in industrial psychology. The establishment of different institutes of management by each organization, such as ATIRA (Ahmedabad Textile and Industrial Research Association), SITRA (South Indian Textile Research Association), SRC (Sri Ram Center for Industrial Relations), and the National Productivity Council, and the gradually increasing contact between academic psychologists and industry have provided the necessary corrective.

Personality. The studies on personality have gradually become more sophisticated, and extensive work has been done in this area. The research work covers assessment techniques, motivation, self-concept, sociocultural factors, learning, perception, psychopharmacology, delinquency, criminality, and abnormal personality.

Military Psychology. This area covers such topics as selection and placement, training, task and work analysis, performance and job satisfaction, display, controls, driving, and safety.

Physiological and Comparative Psychology. This area covers topics such as comparative psychology, natural observation, learning, motivation, social behavior, and sensory processes. In physiological psychology, studies are reported on topics such as brain lesions, brain stimulation, electrical activity, biochemistry, and cardiac and vascular processes.

Social Psychology. The distribution of papers over the last four decades indicates the general trend of social psychological research in India. Prior to 1940 there were only 55 papers covering all eight areas of social psychology. During the next decade (1940–1950) there was little growth in research activities and only 64 papers were published. However, between 1950 and 1960 the number of papers increased to 102 and in the next decade (1960–1970) 306 papers were published.

Methodology and Research Technology. Research work has been done in test construction, validation, and factor analysis. Computer programming is also included as one of the areas of work under methodology. The fator analysis technique is employed in present-day research.

Publications

The main publications are the *Indian Journal of Psychology,* official organ of the Indian Psychological Association; the *Journal of Indian Academy of Applied Psychology,* official organ of the Indian Academy of Applied Psychology; the *Journal of Psychological Research;* the *Indian Journal of Applied Psychology;* and the *Indian Journal of Experimental Psychology.* These are published by the Madras Psychology Society. The psychological studies published by the Universities of Mysore, Manas, and Manaysan are published from Delhi.

Occupational Distribution

The directory of psychologists published by Re Narain (1968) gives a list of psychologists at that time as numbering 734, which by no means may be considered exhaustive. Unfortunately, this is the only reliable source of information. It is seen from this directory that about 31% considered themselves as working in the field of general psychology. The psychologists working in the fields of social, industrial, and educational psychology, mental testing, vocational guidance, and personal-

Table 3. Classification of 734 Indian Psychologists According to Their Major Areas of Interest

Areas	N	Percentage	Rank
Experimental	22	3.0	8
Social	61	8.3	3
General	238	30.8	1
Industrial	46	6.3	4
Vocational guidance	36	4.9	6
Counseling	10	1.4	12
Personality	37	5.1	5
Clinical/abnormal	97	13.2	2
Educational	59	8.1	3
Criminal	12	1.7	10
Mental testing	36	1.0	6
Applied	7	4.6	13
Child	34	4.6	7
Psychometry	14	1.9	9
Psychoanalysis	3	.4	15
Projective techniques	11	.2	11
Parapsychology	1	.2	16
Physiological	4	.6	14
Aesthetics	1	.2	16
Indian psychology	4	.6	14
Agricultural psychology	1	.2	16

ity constitute only 5%. More details may be seen in Table 3, which points to the area of specialization. The picture by 1978 was somewhat different, indicating a growing interest in clinical psychology.

Opportunities for Foreign Psychologists

Entry of foreign psychologists, as with any foreigner, is controlled by the government of India. So far, very few foreign psychologists have been to India on a long-term basis. It may be due partly to the salaries offered them, which are unattractive since institutions in India cannot afford to pay salaries comparable to their own countries. There have been visiting lecturers through the Fullbright scheme, controlled by the United States Education Foundation in India. However, even these have been few and far between.

There may be possibilities in major cities like Bombay, Delhi, Calcutta, and Madras for the independent practice of psychology, but there are currently no particular laws governing this practice.

Indonesia[1]

National Organization

Practically all 500 Indonesian psychologists belong to the Indonesian Psychological Association. The address of the association is:

Indonesian Psychological Association
c/o University of Gajahmada
Faculty of Psychology
Jl. Bulaksumur, Jogjakarta, Indonesia

The official language is Indonesian.

Internal Structure

The coordinating body, due to some constraints of the association, has not yet been active. The chairmanship rotates among the three faculties of psychology (University of Indonesia, Jakarta; University of Pajajaran, Bandung; University of Gajahmada, Jogjakarta) every 4 years.

Membership

The association has approximately 500 members.

Education and Training

The three above-mentioned universities run by the government offer courses in psychology. Also, the Christian Uni-

[1]Based on information supplied by Singgih D. Cunersa, associate dean of academic affairs, Faculty of Psychology, University of Indonesia.

versity of Maranatha, Bandung, has a psychology department. All four universities offer a master's degree; the title usually used after graduation is doctorandus (abbreviated Drs.). Besides this degree, on very rare occasions doctor's degrees in psychology are also awarded. Four doctor's degrees have been granted up to now from the University of Indonesia.

Research

Research is conducted in all universities. The priorities in doing research are in the fields of technology and agriculture and those that are connected with the development of the country. Private research centers are very limited.

Publications

No journal is published by the national psychological organization, but there are other professional journals in Indonesia:

Medical Science, c/o Faculty of Medicine, University of Indonesia, J1. Salemba 4, Jakarata.

Anthropology, c/o Faculty of Literature, University of Indonesia, Rawamangun, Jakarta.

Occupational Distribution

Indonesian psychologists are involved in teaching, research, industrial psychology, vocational guidance, and clinical practice in hospitals and in private.

Opportunities for Foreign Psychologists

Industrial psychologists are more welcome than clinicians in Indonesia, and it is easier to get a job in private than in governmental institutions. Inquiries should be addressed to Indonesian consulates.

Iran[1]

National Organization

The national psychological association is called the
      Psychological Association of Iran
      Kahkshe Amirabad
      24 Esfand Square
      Tehran, Iran
The official languages are Persian, English, and French.

Internal Structure

The governing body of the association, the executive committee, is composed of seven members, namely, chairman, two vice-chairmen, secretary-general, treasurer, and two members, all elected for a period of 2 years.

The aim of the association is "to promote scientific psychology in Iran." Its responsibilities and duties are (1) to expand the scope of psychological research in Iran; (2) to promote the study of psychology and to guide and encourage those choosing to study one of the branches of this science; (3) to organize lectures and seminars on psychological topics; (4) to maintain contact and to cooperate with similar associations, in particular with international associations of psychology; (5) to participate in international conferences and congresses of

[1]Based on information supplied by E. Hashemi, vice-president of Teachers' Training University in Tehran, Iran, and secretary general of the Psychological Association of Iran, and other sources.

psychologists; (6) to publish books, articles, and papers reporting research in psychology; (7) to study and determine the job requirements related to various branches of psychology and to submit necessary proposals to concerned authorities; and (8) to act on any other point that the association finds useful for the promotion of its goals.

Membership

The total number of members is 133, divided into three categories: (1) Regular members should hold a postgraduate degree in psychology, or in related fields, and have publications in psychology. (2) Associate members should hold at least a college degree in psychology or related fields and have an interest in the aims of the association. (3) Honorary members are chosen by the council of the association from among Iranian and foreign scholars with valuable publications in psychology, and persons who have made important contributions to the association.

Education and Training

The first department of psychology in Iran was established at the Teachers' Training University in Tehran in 1959. Three years later a psychology department was organized at the University of Tehran and in a few teachers' training institutions and other schools of higher learning, such as the University of Tabriz, Meshed, and Isfahan. In most cases the study of psychology is related to education and solid work, but the University of Tehran offers courses in clinical psychology and psychotherapy.

The highest degree in psychology is a Ph.D.

Research

The Institute of Education Research and Studies of the Teachers' Training University in Tehran engages in research in educational and developmental psychology. The Institute for Psychological Research and Studies of the University of Tehran conducts research in mental measurements, personnel, and industrial psychology.

Opportunities for Foreign Psychologists

Iran welcomes foreign psychologists, usually on a basis of visiting experts in applied psychology, visiting researchers, and visiting professors. Inquiries should be directed to the

Psychological Association of Iran
Nakhseh Amirabad
24 Esfand Square
Tehran, Iran

Ireland[1]

National Organization

Practically all Irish psychologists are members of the
Psychological Society of Ireland
(Cumann Siceolaithe Eireann)
75 Merrion Square
Dublin 2, Ireland
The official languages are English and Gaelic.

Internal Structure

The society is governed by a council of not fewer than 16 and not more than 20 members, including a president, a president-elect, an honorary secretary, and an honorary treasurer.

Election to the council is by secret ballot, personal or postal, at the annual general meeting. The officers are elected by the council.

Membership

There are 206 members of the society, divided into three categories: (1) fellows—9, (2) associates—33, and (3) graduate members—164.

---

[1]Based on information supplied by James McLoone, honorary secretary of the Psychological Society of Ireland, and other sources.

Membership Requirements

The minimum qualifications for graduate membership is an honors degree in which psychology is a main subject. Associates must have "been successfully engaged for a period of at least 3 years whole time in work in the area of psychology." Fellows must (1) have been engaged in work of a psychological nature for a total period of at least 10 years, (2) possess "an advanced knowledge of psychology in at least one of its aspects," and (3) have "made a significant contribution to the advancement of psychological knowledge or practice."

Major Activities

There is an annual general meeting and 2-day conference in May; average attendance is 75. There is also an autumn conference lasting 4 days.

Lectures and workshops for members are given, as are seminars in association with other professional groups.

The society develops and publishes policy documents, e.g., *A Psychological Service to Schools* (January 1975) and *Psychologists in the Service of Health* (July 1975). Courses in psychology for the general public are given.

Education and Training

Six university colleges offer training in psychology: the National University of Ireland: (1) University College, Dublin, (2) University College, Cork, and (3) University College, Galway; the University of Dublin: (4) Trinity College, Dublin, (5) The Queen's University of Belfast and (6) The New University of Ulster, Coleraine.

All six colleges offer B.A., B.Sc., M.A., M.Sc., M. Psych.Sc., and diploma in psychology (postgraduate). All six colleges grant the Ph.D. degree.

Legal Status

There is no provision for licensing or certification, but the psychological society is currently developing a professional ethical code.

Research

Some psychological research is being done in the psychology and education departments of the universities. There are no private research centers. Most research is carried out in independent research centers, which receive state support, e.g., Educational Research Centre, Economic and Social Research Centre, Irish Institute of Linguistics, Irish Management Institute, Irish Productivity Centre, Institute of Public Administration, Agricultural Institute, and The National Institute for Physical Planning and Construction Research.

Publications

The Irish Journal of Psychology, Woodlands, Renmore, Galway, Ireland, is published irregularly (one or two issues per annum).

The Irish Psychologist, Woodlands, Renmore, Galway, Ireland, is a monthly bulletin.

There are no other strictly psychological journals, but psychological papers appear in other journals, e.g., in the Irish Journal of Education, St. Patrick's College, Dublin 9 (published biannually), and in Social Studies, Maynooth College, Maynooth, Co. Kildare (six issues per annum).

Occupational Distribution

Most Irish psychologists occupy academic (50) and research (20) positions. Educational (20) and clinical (15) psychologists work either in governmental schools and hospitals or in the state-supported voluntary organization.

Opportunities for Foreign Psychologists

Ireland welcomes well-qualified foreign psychologists. Inquiries should be directed to the Psychological Society of Ireland.

Israel[1]

National Organization

The national psychological organization is the
Israel Psychological Association (IPA)
(Histadrut Ha'psichologim Be'Israel)
Department of Psychology
Bar Ilan University
Ramat Gan, Israel

The official language is Hebrew. Nevertheless, English and French documents are accepted. Other languages have to be translated.

Internal Structure

The Israel Psychological Association was founded in 1958 through the union of the Israeli Psychological Association and the Clinical Psychologists' Organisation.

Since 1972 all members of the IPA are also members of the Union of Graduates in Social Sciences and the Humanities, a national professional union of the Labor Federation of Israel. By an agreement between the IPA and the union, the latter takes care of the working conditions of psychologists, their salaries, and matters of labor relations.

[1]Based on information supplied by Mordechai Eran, chairman of the executive committee of the Israel Psychological Association.

123

The major executive body of the IPA is the central committee. Its seven members are elected by the general assembly, which convenes at least once every 2 years. The members of the central committee elect the president, the secretary, and the treasurer. This committee is responsible for the ongoing professional activities of the association, supervision of other committees, maintaining contact with governmental and professional bodies, preparation of special advanced study programs, etc.

The central committee nominates a membership committee, which checks the credentials of applicants for membership. It should be noted that this is quite a difficult and sensitive task in an immigration country like Israel, since it requires the inspection and evaluation of curricula from universities and agencies all over the world.

Membership

The association has 700 members, and there are no categories or levels of membership. However, two of the divisions of the association, the clinical and the educational, do distinguish between "members" and "supervisors." Only the latter may supervise junior psychologists attending a program of specialization.

Divisions

There are at present three divisions in the association: clinical, educational, and social-industrial. Several other divisions (e.g., experimental, rehabilitational, and student counseling) are still in the process of organization (see Table 1).

Membership Requirements

The major requirement for admission to the IPA is a master's degree (or its equivalent) in psychology from a recognized university. The IPA keeps an index of departments of psychology all over the world. (Table 2 shows membership by country

Table 1. Membership in Divisions of the IPA

Division membership	Clinical	Educational	Social-industrial	Other members
Members	176	112	57	289
out of which come				
Supervisors	82	63	—	—

of origin.) Graduates from unknown departments may be admitted if they hold a master's degree in psychology and if their record of studies includes at least 40 yearly hours of psychology, at least half of which are at the master level. The above program must include the following courses: (1) introduction to psychology, (2) learning, perception, or thinking, (3) social psychology, (4) experimental or physiological psychology, (5) developmental psychology, (6) personality or abnormal psychology, (7) statistics, (8) methodology or a research seminar.

Admission to the clinical division requires supervision of at least 200 hours in psychodiagnosis and 200 hours in psychotherapy. This supervision must take place in a recognized institution and by a certified supervisor.

Admission to the educational division is open to any member of the IPA who has acquired: (1) 3 years' experience in a recognized psychological institution, (2) supervision of 200 hours in treatment and counseling, (3) supervision on diagnosis of 50 cases of a wide variety of problems, and (4) acquaintance with the educational system and the institutions of special education (types of institutions and treatment, types of patients, and special diagnostic procedure).

Major Activities

The organization of national conventions is one of the major activities of the IPA. Conventions are held about once every 1½ to 2 years.

Other major activities of the IPA include admission and

Table 2. IPA Members by Country of Origin[a]

Origin	Percentage
Western Europe	15
Eastern Europe	22
North America, Australia, and South Africa	13
South America	10
Asia and Africa	3
Israel	37

[a]These statistics pertain to membership as of 1976. Since then membership has increased by 100 new members. Hence, the present distributions should include a higher percentage of younger, Israeli-born psychologists.

supervision of the work of new members. The IPA is interested in facilitating the assimilation of immigrant psychologists, and cooperates with governmental agencies for this purpose.

The IPA organizes (often in cooperation with other bodies, such as the Union of Graduates in the Social Sciences and the Humanities, and the Ministry of Education) advanced courses and seminars. These courses are designed mainly to acquaint members with, and develop skills in, modern treating methods, e.g., behavior modification, psychodrama, and family therapy.

The IPA represents Israeli psychologists in public and governmental institutions. For instance, the IPA takes part in the formulation of laws pertaining to the work of psychologists.

The IPA provides its members with information pertaining to psychology, psychological research, and psychologists in the country. The major channels of communication are publications (including reports, memoranda, and lists of members) of the association.

The IPA represents Israel's psychologists in international bodies. It is a member of the International Union of Psychological Science.

Education and Training

Training in psychology is offered by six major institutions: Bar Ilan University in Ramat Gan, Ben Gurion University in

Beer-Sheba, Haifa University in Haifa, the Hebrew University in Jerusalem, the Technion in Haifa, and Tel Aviv University in Tel Aviv. In addition, all teachers' colleges in the country offer courses in general and educational psychology.

Basic training in psychology and a bachelor's degree in this field are provided by the departments of psychology in Bar Ilan, Haifa, Tel Aviv, and the Hebrew universities. Ben Gurion University offers a B.A. in behavioral sciences with an optional focus on psychology.

Programs of graduate training are offered by all these institutions except Ben Gurion University:

1. Bar Ilan University offers a master's program in each of the following areas: clinical, educational, rehabilitational, social, industrial, and experimental-physiological psychology. The department also admits a limited number of doctoral candidates.

2. Haifa University has a program leading to an M.A. in psychology in clinical, social, and experimental-physiological psychology.

3. The master's program of the Hebrew University in Jerusalem focuses on three areas: general, clinical, and educational psychology. An additional program is offered by the Department of Psychology and the School of Education, which provides training in educational psychology for purposes other than treatment of individuals (e.g., social school psychologists, curriculum development).

4. The Technion provides two options for graduate training in psychology: in the Faculty of Industrial Engineering and Management, it provides training mostly in applied psychology. The second program is available at the Haifa School of Medicine and trains students for M.Sc. and Ph.D. in medical sciences in behavioral biology, neuropsychology, and physiological psychology. The two latter programs are not recognized by the IPA.

5. The Department of Psychology in Tel Aviv University offers graduate programs in clinical, clinical-educational, social, occupational, and general-experimental psychology.

6. A postgraduate training program is available at Tel-Aviv University, the School of Advanced Studies in Medicine.

This program grants a diploma in psychotherapy for clinical psychologists, psychiatric social workers, and psychiatrists.

7. A similar postgraduate course in psychotherapy is organized by the Israeli Psychoanalytic Society in Jerusalem. This society provides an advanced program in psychoanalysis.

Legal Status

So far, only the clinical and the educational divisions have rules that restrict practice (in their respective fields) to members of the divisions. These rules have been ratified by the IPA and are therefore obligatory for all members of the IPA. It should be noted, however, that so far a legally recognized certification of psychologists does not exist. While the IPA supervises the practice of psychology by its members, there is no way to control practice of nonmembers.

Research

Each of the university departments has its own research facilities (mostly laboratories, measurement equipment, and sometimes a clinic). Some of the research done in these departments is organized in institutes of the universities. However, most of the work is done by individual researchers. The major resources for funds are large foundations (such as the Ford Foundation and the Israeli Academy of Sciences) and internal funds of the universities. Some of the institutes associated with departments are the Institute for the Study of Sleep and Dreams in Bar Ilan University, the Human Development Center at the Hebrew University, and the Center for Psychology at the Technion.

Public research facilities perform much of the large-scale research in the behavioral sciences in Israel. These organizations perform studies for the government and other public organizations, as well as for individual researchers.

Notable among these are (1) the Institute for Applied Social Research, which works especially in the field of social psychology and public opinion; (2) the Henrietta Szold Institute for Research in the Behavioral Sciences, which performs many studies in the fields of educational and social psychology; (3) the Hadassah Vocational Training Institute, whose researchers work mainly on development of tests; (4) the Hadassah-Wizo Canada Research Institute, which specializes in research on instrumental enrichment and the education of environmentally deprived children.

Publications

The IPA publishes a journal entitled *Psychology*, devoted to the dissemination of general information and to the exchange of opinions.

Megamot, a quarterly journal published by the Henrietta Szold Institute, is the major journal of the behavioral sciences.

Hachinuch (Education) and *Chavat D'at* (Opinion), edited by the Ministry of Education, are both journals in the field of educational psychology.

Psychologists often publish their papers in the *Israel Journal of Medical Sciences* and in the *Israel Annals of Psychiatry*.

Table 3. Type of Work Done and Percentage of Psychologists in Each Category[a]

	Percentage
University professors and instructors	32
School psychologists—guidance and counseling	83
Rehabilitation and general hospital psychologists	4
Clinical psychologists	27
Private practitioners	2
Research psychologists	6
Industrial psychologists	4
Others	4

[a]The columns add up to more than 100% since many of the respondents indicated more than one job.

Most of the papers of Israeli psychologists are published abroad, in European and American journals.

Occupational Distribution

The percentage of psychologists in each category studied is shown in Table 3.

Opportunities for Foreign Psychologists

Israel, as an immigration country, is used to absorbing professionals trained in other countries. Each applicant to the IPA must submit his educational record. The IPA is trying to organize special courses and seminars for immigrant psychologists in order to acquaint the newcomers with Israel, its problems, and the generally used professional methods.

Inquiries should be directed to the Israeli consulates.

Italy[1]

Introduction

Italian contributions to psychology go back to the 19th century, to the work of C. Lombroso (1876), R. Ardigo (1870), Mosso (1884), and many others. The first Italian psychological journal, *Rivista di Psicologìa*, was established by G. C. Ferrari in 1905. Between 1910 and 1945 the old universities in Rome, Florence, and Turin, and the new ones in Padua and Milan actively pursued psychological studies in several fields and in diverse points of view, such as positivism, foundationalism, Gestalt, behaviorism, and psychoanalysis.

At the present time, Italian psychologists actively pursue all aspects of psychological research and practice.

National Organization

The name and address of the Italian psychological association are as follows:

Società Italiana di Psicologìa Scientìfica (SIPS)
c/o Istituto di Psicologìa, Città Universitària
00100 Roma
Italy

The official language is Italian.

---

[1]Based on information supplied by Prof. Luigi Meschieri of the University of Rome, on behalf of the Società Italiana di Psicologìa Scientìfica (SIPS); and other sources.

Internal Structure

The Italian society (SIPS) is governed by the executive committee and the president, chosen in general elections held every 2 years. The executive committee's major responsibilities are (1) to screen membership applications; (2) to organize the society's national conventions; (3) to promote and oversee cooperative relations among the SIPS and other psychological organizations—Italian, foreign, and international; (4) to supervise publication of *Rivista di Psicologìa,* the SIPS official journal; and (5) to foster research and evaluate training and other national activities in the field of psychology.

The regional coordinating committees promote professional contacts among psychologists in their respective geographical areas, as well as in particular branches of scientific or professional psychology.

The executive committee is composed of five members. Of the four elected members, at least two must be practicing psychologists (as distinct from psychologists whose main field of activity is academic work).

The past president is the fifth member, ex officio.

Membership

At present the SIPS has 800 full members and it is contemplating establishing a new category of "adherents" (e.g., university students in psychology, scholars in surrounding disciplines).

The 800 members are nominally divided into two sections: professional (55%) and academic (45%).

Membership Requirements

Under Article L of the SIPS bylaws, the following are eligible for membership: (1) university full professors in psychology; (2) holders of a Ph.D. (libera docenza) in psychology; (3) holders of a bachelor's degree in psychology, or holders of a bachelor's degree in a field other than psychology who have completed 3 years of postgraduate work in psychology at a state or state-accredited university; (4) full-time university instructors of psychology; (5) part-time teaching assistants who have held such a position for at least 2 years; (6) university graduates in related fields (education, philosophy, medicine, sociology, etc.) employed full time as psychologists on the staff of national or local public agencies or of permanent and officially recognized research centers; (7) holders of a Ph.D. or bachelor's degree in psychology from foreign universities; (8) university graduates in related fields (education, philosophy, medicine, sociology, etc.) with long supervised experience as psychologists in private practice or private employment and whose specific competence (eventually ascertained with personal interview and examination) meets the requirements and special standards set by the executive committee.

Major Activities

The major activities of the SIPS are the National Convention of Italian Psychologists, held every 2 to 3 years; publication of the quarterly, *Rivista di Psicologìa;* and publication of a bimonthly newsletter for the membership.

Other Psychological Organizations

There are other national scientific and professional associations dealing with psychology, among them: Associazione per la Psicologìa Italiana del Lavoro (APIL), Associazione Italiana degli Psicologi Professionisti (AIPP), Società Italiana di Psicoanàlisi, Associazione Italiana di Psicologìa Analìtica, Società Italiana Rorschach e altre techniche prioettive, Società Italiana di Psicologìa Individuale, and Società Italiana di Psicologìa dello Sport.

Education and Training

In the 35 state-recognized universities, there are some 250 cattedre (chairs) of psychology and/or its branches held by full professors (50%) or by part-time yearly appointed professors. Each professor is usually helped by one to five full-time assistants or more. These cattedre, when located in the same university in groups of three or more, can be organized within an istituto di psicologìa (department of psychology). These institutes are mainly established inside the faculties of magistero (similar to teachers' colleges or departments of education) and, in a decreasing number, at the faculties of philosophy, medicine, and political, social, statistical, and economic sciences. A few isolated cattedre are also in the faculties of law, foreign languages, and natural sciences, in the physical education colleges, nursing colleges, and schools for social assistance. The last three, however, do not reach a university status and have no assistants. Due to the different aims and their location, less than half of the total number of cattedre of higher education deal with introductory courses in general psychology; the others are elevated to specific subject matters (e.g., developmental, clinical, social, physiological, industrial, dynamic, and experimental psychology).

The Italian universities offer two different degrees in psychology:

1. The diplòma di làurea in psicologìa, awarded upon successful completion of a 4-year course of studies, was started recently at the state universities of Rome and Padua. The holder of this degree is officially certified as a dottore in psicologia.

2. The diplòma di specializzazione in general psychology or its specialized fields (e.g., medical, educational, clinical, industrial) is a postgraduate degree awarded upon successful completion of a 3-year course of practical and theoretical studies at an accredited university. Admission to this last course of studies is limited to holders of a bachelor's degree (làurea) in psychology or related fields.

Nondegree certificates are issued by a variety of universities, public agencies, and private organizations for attendance of unofficial training courses, seminars, etc., lasting from a few days up to a year. Depending on the circumstances, these sources are attended by undergraduate and postgraduate students, working psychologists, teachers, social workers, physicians, judges, etc.

Nonuniversity centers offer training particularly in psychotherapy. The standards of these courses vary widely, from internationally recognized orthodox Freudian training to newly established courses run by private centers and individuals whose professional and technical standards are questionable.

There are nearly 20,000 students registered in the 4-year course leading to the diplòma di làurea in psicologìa. The bulk of these students is to be found in the first 2 years of the course, due to the exceedingly high dropout rate. The number of students enrolled at any one time in the 3-year course leading to the diplòma di specializzazione in psicologìa fluctuates considerably because universities do not necessarily offer this course every year and, when they do, they put a ceiling on enrollment (numerus clausus). Currently, between three and five schools work simultaneously, each admitting from 20 to 100 students. In any given year—with a decreasing trend—about 100 students complete the 3-year course and are awarded the diplòma di specializzazione in psicologìa.

Legal Status

Governmental supervision of accreditation is only indirect and is exercised through the Ministry of Education, which reviews and approves the degree curricula worked out by the university's psychology departments. Even this indirect control has been attenuated since 1970, however, because students are now allowed to choose among many optional courses within the required number of credits.

As for governmental regulation of professional accreditation, a bill is now before Parliament with a view to establishing a national order of psychologists. Under the provisions of this bill—as for other professions—candidates will have to pass a psychology board examination to obtain a license.

Research

The Italian National Research Council (CNR) has its own Institute of Psychology with an estimated yearly operating budget of 600 million Italian liras (nearly 500 million for personnel and nearly 100 million for equipment and premises). It is staffed by about 40 full-time graduate researchers and technicians, plus 7 secretaries and administrators. The CNR's Institute of Psychology is housed in Rome (Via dei Monti Tiburtini 509, 00157 Roma) in a five-story building and is endowed with rather sophisticated scientific equipment and a library of nearly 7,000 volumes and more than 200 collections of scientific journals. Its activity concentrates on basic research and, more recently, on certain fields of applied psychology such as education, psycholinguistics, rehabilitation of the handicapped, and other areas.

Given the number of students crowding the universities and the extremely high student-to-faculty ratio, the university-based research activity is seriously cut back. Exceptions are the large state universities of Padua, Milan, Bologna, Rome, and Genoa, a few smaller state-run institutions of higher learning, and, among the nongovernmental universities, the Catholic University at Milan and Rome and the Pontificio Ateneo Salesiano of Rome. All of the above have good libraries and are endowed with more or less sophisticated laboratory equipment; in most cases, moreover, they have access to computer services and data-processing centers when they do not have their own computer. A few institutes of psychology associated with medical faculties also have access to patients' wards and ambulatory facilities. Traditionally, each of these institutes specializes in some particular field of research. These are, respectively, Padua, perception and psychometrics; Milan, industrial and clinical psychology; Genoa, child psychology; Catholic University, clinical and dynamic psychology; Ateneo Salesiano, educational psychology. In addition to the small amount of money allocated to them by university budgets, the various departments of psychology can also receive funds from applied research under contracts with private and public agencies. Occasionally, they also receive grants for specific projects from the Italian Research Council and from international or foreign organizations and foundations.

Research in applied psychology is sponsored by corporate research centers devoted mainly to in-company questions (e.g., personnel selection and classification, training, labor, and public relations), operated by a number of large private companies (e.g., Fiat, Montedison, Pirelli), publicly owned or controlled companies of the State Holdings System (e.g., Finsider, Alitalia), and state-owned public utilities (e.g., Italcable, National Telephone System).

Both the National Agency for Accident Prevention and, on a smaller scale, the Italian State Railways have a central research unit and sectional laboratories mainly devoted to personnel selection and training, public relations propaganda, and marketing research. RAI-TV, Italy's state-controlled radio and television broadcasting network, has its own research and information center for continuous or special audience opinion polls.

Publications

Journals. There are nine major psychological journals in Italy:

Rivista di Psicologìa, founded in 1905, is published quarterly by Giunti-Barbera, Via Gioberti 34, 50136 Firenze.

Archìvio di Psicologìa, Neurologìa, Psichiatrìa, is published quarterly by Largo A. Gemelli, 1, 20123 Milano.

Bollettino di Psicologìa Applicata is a periodical, publishing six numbers per year at Via R. Franchi, 5, 50137 Firenze.

Giornale Italiano di Psicologìa/Italian Journal of Psychology is published quarterly by Il Mulino Editore, Via S. Stefano 6, 40125 Bologna.

Rivista di Psicologìa Analìtica is published twice a year, c/o Marsilio Editori, Santa Croce 518/z, 30125 Venezia.

Rivista di Psicologìa Individuale is a periodical published at Piazza Irnerio 2, 20146 Milano.

Rivista di Psicoanàlisi is published every 4 months, c/o Pensièro Scientìfico, Via Panoma 48, 00198 Roma.
Psicologìa e Lavoro is published bimonthly at Via S. Valeria 5, Milano.
Rivista di Psicologìa e Sociale is published quarterly at Via A. Rosmini, 5, Torino.

Many technical articles of psychology are published, as well, in a wide range of scientific and professional journals of sociology, philosophy, medicine and its branches, especially psychiatry, criminology, education, economics, and industrial and administrative management.

Books. Italy publishes a great many books in psychology, both original works and translations. A partial list of publishers follows:

Angeli, Viale Monza 106, 20127 Milano (manuals, readings)

Armando, Via della Gensola 60, 00153 Roma (general, clinical, educational)

Astrolabio-Ubaldini, Via G. d'Arezzo 16, 00198 Roma (psychoanalysis)

Boringhieri, Corso V. Emanuele 86, 10121 Torino

Bulzoni, Via Liburni 14, 00185 Roma

Einaudi, Via Biancamano 1, 10121 Torino

Etas Libri, Via Bixio 30, 20129 (industrial, social)

Feltrinelli, Via Andegari 6, 20121 Milano (social, clinical)

Garzanti, Via Senato 25, 20121 Milano

Giunti-Barbera, Via Scipione Ammirato, 37, 50136 Firenze

Martello, Piazza del Liberty 4, 20121 Milano

Mulino, Via S. Stefano 6, 40125 Bologna (social, methods)

Nuova Italia, Via Giacomini 9, 50132 Firenze (educational, developmental)

Organizzazioni Speciali, Via R. Franchi 5, 50137 Firenze (tests, apparatus, diagnostic manuals)

La Scuola, Via Cadorna 11, 25100 Brescia (educational, developmental)

Sociatà Editrice Internazionale (SEI), Corso Regina Mar-
gherita 176, 10152 Torino
Vita e Pensièro, Largo A. Gemelli 1, 20123 Milano

Occupational Distribution

The number of positions in psychology is highly uncertain,
for it depends on (1) the future level of national income and
political organization; (2) the official recognition of the profession and the establishment of a national order of psychologists;
(3) the policy in progress to transfer from central to local authorities some duties involving public health, education, professional training, territory, and social organization; (4) the reform
of the universities of the secondary schools; and (5) the possibility of substituting an estimated 25% of positions already held
provisionally by nonqualified workers.

Most Italian psychologists occupy teaching positions in
universities and high schools. A great many work in mental
hygiene centers, child guidance clinics, and in industrial
psychology.

Opportunities for Foreign Psychologists

There are official regulations and standards governing the
recognition of foreign academic degrees and curricula. There is
no regulation of foreign-trained private practitioners, a number
of whom are working in Italy. The job market will be, in the
near future, overcrowded.

Inquiries should be directed to Italian consulates.

Japan[1]

Introduction

Psychology has been a well-established branch of scientific research for at least 100 years. It was originally influenced by British and American scholars; Yuiro Motora, who studied at Boston University and Johns Hopkins University, was appointed in 1888, the first lecturer in psychophysics at the Tokyo University. In 1903 the first two psychological laboratories were established by Matsamuto.

From its inception, Japanese psychology emphasized the experimental approach. Experimental studies followed in Wundt's footsteps, and in the 1920s Gestalt psychology exercised significant influence.

After World War II, the Japanese higher education rapidly expanded. In 1960 the total number of schools of higher learning in Japan was close to 550; in 1978 it was over 900. In 1960 about 200 schools of higher learning offered training in psychology; in 1976 their number had grown to over 400.

Experimental psychology, with special emphasis on sensation, perception, learning, and memory, seems to continue to be the prevalent area of interest for Japanese psychologists.

[1]Based on information supplied by Drs. Shinkuro Iwahara and H. Minami, board of directors, Japanese Psychological Association, and other sources.

National Organization

The main association of Japanese psychologists is the
Japanese Psychological Association
37-13-802, Honga 4 chome, Bunkyo-ku
Tokyo, 113, Japan
The official language is Japanese.
The ruling body of the association is the standing board of
directors.

Membership

Twenty-six hundred psychologists belong to the association. They comprise four categories: (1) regular members—
2,515, (2) foreign members—60, (3) honorary members—7,
(4) supporting members—18.

The divisions are (1) thinking, perception, physiological
psychology—172 members; (2) development, education—654
members; (3) personality, clinical, and criminal psychology—
689 members; (4) cultural, social, and industrial psychology—
354 members; (5) methods, measurement, history, general
psychology—46 members.

Membership Requirements

In order to be admitted to regular membership, applicants
should have a sufficient knowledge of psychology and related
fields. The application for membership is to be forwarded to the
standing board of directors. In order to be admitted to honorary
membership, one must contribute significantly to the association and be elected through the recommendation of the board
of directors and approved by the general assembly.

There are also supporting members, who contribute financially to the association and who will be elected by the approval
of the standing board of directors.

Other Psychological Organizations

In addition to the Japanese Psychological Association, there are organizations devoted to particular aspects of psychology as a science and as a profession, namely, the Japanese Association of Educational Psychology, the Japanese Society of Social Psychology, the Japanese Society of Animal Psychology, the Japanese Society for Group Dynamics, the Japanese Association for Psychoanalysis, the Japanese Association for Clinical Psychology, the Japanese Association of Aviation Medicine and Psychology, and the Japanese Association of Applied Psychology.

Education and Training

Out of the over 900 Japanese schools of higher learning, 175 provide graduate studies, and of 400 schools of higher learning where psychology is taught, only 20 offer graduate programs in various fields of psychology.

These universities are Ayokama Gakuin in Tokyo, Doshida in Hiroshima, Hokkaido in Sapporo, International Christian in Tokyo, Keio in Tokyo, Komazawa in Tokyo, Kwansei Gakuin in Nashinomaya, Kyoto in Kyoto, Kyushu in Fukuoka, Nagoia in Nagoia, Nihon in Tokyo, Osaka City in Osaka, Ritsumeikan in Kyoto, Tohoku in Sendal, Tokyo in Tokyo, Tokyo Educational in Tokyo, Tokyo Metropolitan in Tokyo, Waseda in Tokyo.

Japanese universities offer B.A. degrees (gakushi) at the completion of undergraduate studies and M.A. (shushi) and Ph.D. (hakushi) degrees. Graduate students may specialize in any aspect of psychology, such as experimental, social, comparative, personality, developmental, educational, clinical, industrial, and physiological.

Research

The National Institute for Mental Health, established in 1952, carries on research in several fields of psychology, especially diagnostic methods and psychotherapy. The National Educational Research Institute engages in research in mental measurements, student guidance, etc. The Research Institute of Labor Science conducts research in industrial and engineering psychology.

The Japanese universities are heavily involved in basic research in learning and memory, sensation and perception, mathematical, physiological, and comparative psychology, and increasingly also in developmental, social, and clinical psychology. Japanese psychology plays a highly significant role in international psychological research.

Publications

Two journals are published by the Japanese Psychological Association: The *Japanese Journal of Psychology,* a bimonthly, and *Japanese Psychological Research,* a quarterly.

The *Japanese Journal of Educational Psychology,* a quarterly, is published by the Japanese Association of Educational Psychology, c/o Faculty of Educational Psychology, University of Tokyo, Tokyo, Japan.

The *Annual of Animal Psychology* is published by the Japanese Society for Animal Psychology, c/o the Department of Psychology, University of Tokyo, Tokyo, Japan.

The *Japanese Journal of Experimental Social Psychology* is published semiannually by the Japanese Group Dynamics Association, c/o the Faculty of Education, Kyushu University, Hakasaki Higashi-ku, Fukuoka, Japan.

Occupational Distribution

Most Japanese psychologists occupy academic positions as professors and research workers, with a prevalence of experimental and educational studies. In 1947 and 1948 Japan issued child and juvenile welfare laws, and since then a great many psychologists work in welfare agencies and child guidance and vocational guidance centers. There has been a continuous increase in the need for the services of clinical psychologists in clinics and hospitals. Some Japanese psychologists are engaged in industrial psychology and in governmental agencies.

Opportunities for Foreign Psychologists

Foreign psychologists interested in conducting research in Japan or in a temporary appointment to a Japanese university should contact a particular university or the Japanese Cultural Affairs Bureau of the Ministry of Foreign Affairs in Tokyo, Japan.

Korea[1]

National Organization

The official name and address of the national psychological organization are as follows:

Korean Psychological Association (KPA)
Department of Psychology, College of Social Sciences
Seoul National University
Seoul, 151, Korea

The official language is Korean.

Internal Structure

According to the new constitution, which went into effect early in 1975, the association's ruling bodies are the executive committee, the council of representatives, and divisional committees.

Executive Committee. This comprises the president (elected), who designates a chief executive officer, a publicity officer, a finance officer, a membership officer, a general affairs officer, and the chief editor of the *Journal of Korean Psychological Association*.

Council of Representatives. This consists of the president, the division presidents, the heads of psychology departments (ex officio), and representatives from organizations employing or representing a sizable number of KPA members or from regional groups (president-designees).

[1]Based on information supplied by Jae-ho Cha, chief executive officer of the Korean Psychological Association, and other sources.

Divisions. The officers are the president (elected), the division representative, two editors of the *Journal of Korean Psychological Association* (all designated by the division president), and officers, the number of whom varies from division to division.

Electoral System. The president is elected by the members at the annual convention. Division presidents are elected by respective division members.

Membership

Membership of the KPA totals close to 200. These members fall into categories of regular and affiliate members. Their divisions are clinical and counseling psychology and industrial psychology.

Membership Requirements

For regular membership a bachelor's or higher degree in psychology is required.

Affiliate status requires work in the field of psychology and recommendations from two regular members. The application must be reviewed and approved by the council of representatives.

For division membership the two divisions have no special requirements other than membership in the association and interest in joining a division.

Major Activities

An annual convention is held in October each year. The convention programs usually include paper presentations and a general meeting of the association, which elects the president and considers activity and fiscal reports.

The executive committee meets at least bimonthly to discuss its affairs. It may meet in an expanded meeting, in which case the usual committee is joined by division representatives.

The association publishes the *Journal of Korean Psychological Association* and the bimonthly *Korean Psychological Association Newsletter.*

Education and Training

Three universities have departments of psychology; one has a department of educational psychology and another a department of industrial psychology.

B.A. and M.A. degrees in psychology are conferred at Seoul National University, Korea University, Sung'gyun'kwan University, Ewha Women's University, and Chung'ang University. The Ph.D. degree is granted by the Seoul National University, Korea University, and Sung'gyun'kwan University.

Legal Status

The Division of Clinical and Counseling Psychology issues certificates for clinical psychologists and counseling psychologists to those KPA members whose performance on written examinations is judged satisfactory and who show evidence of required experience in their respective professions. The division's certification procedure recognizes two levels of expertise in each profession. None of these certifications has recently initiated moves aimed at legalization of practices of clinical and counseling psychologists.

Research

Government Agencies. The following are engaged in research: Aviation Medicine Research Center, Republic of Korea Air Force; National Railroad Bureau; Selective Service Bureau; Research Committee of Juvenile Delinquency, National Council on Protection of Juveniles.

University-Connected Facilities. Some of the problems that are being studied or that have been studied include ego identity in student populations, attitude measurement, lan-

guage development, verbal learning, conformity, son preference attitude, origin of achievement motive, and effect of gin-
seng on animal behavior. A sizable number of studies were
concerned with developing psychological tests or scales. Professors' research is usually funded by Ministry of Education
grants and by private foundations, of which there are about half
a dozen in Seoul.

Private Research Centers. Korean Institute for Research in the Behavioral Sciences, Manpower Development
Research Institute, and Industrial Health Centers all support
ongoing research.

Publications

The association's official journal is the *Journal of Korean
Psychological Association,* minimum of two issues a year. Its
address is the same as that of the association.

Other professional journals are *Research Bulletin, Research Notes,* and *Psychological Studies in Population Family
Planning.* All are published by the Korean Institute for Research
in the Behavioral Sciences, Seoul, Korea.

Occupational Distribution

Many Korean psychologists are employed as guidance
counselors in schools and universities, as clinical psychologists
in hospitals, and as university professors. There is a growing
interest in industrial psychology.

Opportunities for Foreign Psychologists

Korean nationals with a Ph.D. or its equivalent have a
fairly good chance of getting a full-time appointment with an
existing or yet-to-be-established department of psychology or
with a department in a related field. There are still many large
universities without a department of psychology. These are all
potential employers of qualified psychologists. Foreign-trained
psychologists are few in number in Korea at this time and,

therefore, there is a definite demand for them, although such demands may not immediately be translated into action. Inquiries should be addressed to a particular university.

Lebanon[1]

Introduction

There is no national psychological organization in Lebanon. The Lebanese National Science Association does not include psychology among its disciplines. The Lebanese National Science Foundation restricts its grants to the natural sciences and does not ordinarily consider psychological studies to fall in the category of natural science.

Education and Training

There are five institutions of higher education in Lebanon that offer training in psychology. The American University of Beirut established a separate department of psychology in 1952. It offers the B.A. and M.A. degrees in psychology following the curriculum of American universities. Each year in the 1970s the department awarded from 10 to 20 bachelor's degrees and about half as many master's degrees.

The Ecole Superieur des Lettres is associated with the Université de Lyons, France, and its certificates are approved by that university. It offers the license in psychology and additional graduate work, which permit a student to complete a doctorate with 1 year of residence at the Université de Lyons.

The Université de Saint Joseph gave the license in

[1]Based on information supplied by Edwin Terry Prothro, professor of psychology, University of California.

psychology during the 1960s, but in the early 1970s it began to reduce the scope of its curriculum and dropped the license in psychology. Some psychology courses are still offered. The National Lebanese University offers certificates in psychology in the Faculty of Arts and the Faculty of Pedagogy. The highest degree is the license in psychology.

The Arab University of Beirut is affiliated with the University of Alexandria, Egypt; it offers courses in psychology that lead to a license.

Research

Virtually all of the psychological research done in Lebanon is carried out by professors in the institutions of higher education. Even visiting research scholars supported by agencies outside Lebanon usually affiliate with one of the Lebanese institutions while conducting research. A majority of the professors of psychology in Lebanon were trained in Europe or America.

Lebanon has no journals that are restricted to articles on psychological subjects, but several institutions publish research journals that accept articles of a psychological nature. *Al-Abhath* (Research), the quarterly journal of the Faculty of Arts and Science of the American University of Beirut and *Travaux et Jours,* the monthly journal of the Université de Saint Joseph, publish occasional psychological articles of general interest.

Occupational Distribution

The number of psychologists employed outside of colleges and universities is small. The government employs a few in welfare agencies, and some of the international agencies, with headquarters in Lebanon, employ psychologists as specialists in social science. Generally speaking, however, psychologists are seen as educators. The number of persons working as full-time psychologists is probably not more than 30.

Opportunities for Foreign Psychologists

Lebanese universities welcome foreign psychologists as visiting professors and researchers. Inquiries must be directed to a particular university.

Malta[1]

There are no organizations for the psychological professions in Malta, as the number of practicing psychologists (two) does not warrant the establishment of such societies. The psychologists in the education department were trained in the United Kingdom and/or Canada and are affiliated with British and/or Canadian psychological associations—e.g., the British Psychological Society, the Ontario Psychological Association. The two psychologists both work in the school system.

[1]Based on information supplied by J. V. Spiteri, honorary consul of Malta in New York.

Mexico[1]

Introduction

In the second part of the 19th century, there was the strong liberal influence in the Mexican government that had been crystallized by Benito Juárez. Gabino Barreda, a Mexican educator who studied under A. Comte, believed that positivism was the best doctrine and he organized Mexican education accordingly. Justo Sierra, the minister of education, provided the opportunity for Ezequiel A. Chávez, probably the first Mexican psychologist, to request the inclusion of a course of psychology in the escuela preparatoría. Ezequiel A. Chávez was nominated founder and first professor of a course in psychology at the preparatory school in 1893. The preparatoría covers the 9th to the 12th grade of education, and since the course in psychology was offered in the 11th grade and has remained in the curriculum ever since, it is probable that Mexico is a pioneer in the teaching of psychology at the high school level.

Chávez was particularly influenced by Ribot, James, Titchener, McDougall, James Mark Baldwin, Pierre Janet, George Dumas, and Spencer. He was an enthusiast, and through his efforts Mark Baldwin spent the years from 1909 to 1913 in Mexico. It is said that Baldwin wrote his books entitled *Psychology and Sociology* and the *History of Psychology* in Mexico. At this time, psychology in Mexico was very much up-to-date.

[1]Based on information supplied by R. Díaz-Guerrero, research professor, Faculty of Psychology, Universidad Nacional Autónoma de México, and president, INCCAPAC.

Although brought in by reformation, the positivistic trend grew in strength under the dictatorship of Porfirio Díaz. The Mexican revolution in 1910 went strongly against positivism in philosophy and education and its influence in psychology. In 1938, when the career of psychology was inaugurated at the Faculty of Philosophy and Letters of the Universidad Nacional Autónoma de México, Wundt's theories were taught as if they represented the latest advances in psychology. Refugees from the Spanish civil war, however, brought to Mexico Dilthey, Spranger, and Gestalt psychology.

During the 1940s, almost all teachers of psychology were physicians, psychiatrists, or philosophers. The 1950s were influenced by Freudian and Frommian psychoanalysts. During the 1960s, R. Díaz-Guerrero and a number of young psychologists prepared an academic revolution that provided the background for understanding the present status of psychology in Mexico.

From 1962, in a period of 13 years, psychology has moved all the way from a philosophical orientation to experimental design, from an exclusively psychoanalytical psychology for clinical practice to a variety of forms with particular accent on behavior modification, from an exclusively academically oriented department to a professional school, from an accent on individual psychology to an equal accent on the individual in social environment.

National Organizations

The main national organization of psychologists in Mexico is the Sociedad Mexicana de Psicología, A.C., founded in 1950. The official address of the association is Filadélfia 119–202, México 18, D.F., telephone 593-45-82.

In the last 10 years other associations have grown out of the specific interests of their members. Thus, there is the Sociedad Mexicana de Psiología Clínica, A.C. The official address of the association is Insurgentes Sur 682-101, México 12, D.F., telephone: 523-28-58.

The Asociación de Psicólogos Industriales, A.C., has its address at Yucatán 20, Mezzanine 1, México 7, D.F. The Asociación Nacional de Psicólogos del Sector Público, A.C. (Public Service), has its address in Puebla 398-502, México 11, D.F. Finally, the Consejo Nacional para la Enseñanza e Investigación en Psicología is an association of departments of psychology, with its address at Facultad de Psicología, Ciudad Universitaria, México 20, D.F. The Sociedad Mexicana de Psicología, A.C., a member of the International Union of Scientific Psychology, has recently modified its bylaws in order to democratize itself further and to permit affiliation by the other societies. The Society of Clinical and Industrial Psychology and the Society for Psychologists in the Public Service have at present applied for affiliation to the Sociedad Mexicana de Psicología, A.C.

Education and Training

After completion of the preparatory grades, the student is admitted to a university career, which at the present time is called the professional level. After 4 or 5 years of professional level studies the student receives the degree of psychologist or licenciado en psicología. The Faculty of Psychology of the Universidad Nacional Autónoma de México also provides master and Ph.D. level studies. Only a few other universities offer the master's degree and most of them only the professional degree.

At present there are 16 departments of psychology in Mexico: (1) Escuela de Psicología, Universidad Anahuac; (2) Departmento de Psicología, Universidad de las Américas; this is the only university that has American training and it offers a bachelor's degree in psychology and a master's degree; (3) Academia de Psicología, Universidad Autónoma del Estado de México; (4) Escuela de Psicología, Universidad Autónoma del Estado de Morelos; (5) Escuel de Psicología, Universidad Autónoma de Guadalajara; (6) Escuela de Psicología, Universidad Autónoma de Nuevo León; (7) Escuela de Psicología, Universidad Autónoma de Puebla; (8) Escuela de Psicología, Universidad Autónoma de San Luis Potosi; (9) Escuela de Psicología, Universidad de Yucatán; (10) Escuela de Psicología, Universidad de Guadalajara; (11) Departamento de Psicología, Universidad Iberoamericana; (12) Departamento de Psicología, Universidad de Monterrey; (13) Facultad de Psicología, Universidad Nacional Autónama de México; (14) Escuela de Psicología, Universidad Veracruzana; (15) Escuela de Psicología, Instituto Tecnólogico y de Estudios Superiores de Occidente; and (16) Carrera de Psicología, Escuela Nacional de Estudios Profesionales, U.N.A.M., Iztacala.

In 1956 there were 200 students in psychology at the National University of Mexico; in 1963, there were 623; in 1966, 1,096; in 1972, close to 3,000. In 1978 close to 5,000 students were enrolled for the professional degree at the Faculty of Psychology of the National University of Mexico. However, the master's and doctor's degrees have been considered extremely specialized education, which should be attempted only by the best of students and particularly those that want to go on to an academic or research career. The number of students that are admitted at this level is reasonably small and there is an increasing and sophisticated faculty to guide the development of the student at this level.

Legal Status

In 1975 the Mexican government legally recognized the profession of psychology. However, the definition of this field is still in process. Up to this time, psychologists have exercised their profession on the basis of the legal degree provided them by the universities. Neither state nor federal professional boards exist to enact special examinations for the practice of psychology.

Research

Before the 1960s, outside of some test standardization and the work of a few isolated individuals like Hernández Peón, there was practically no organized research in psychology in Mexico. In the early 1960s, the Centro de Investigaciónes en Ciencias del Comportamiento (CICC) was formed. The center was the predecessor of the Instituto Nacional de Ciencias del Comportamiento y de la Actitud Pública, A.C. (INCCAPAC), which, in line with its predecessor, has produced internationally recognized multivariate research in the areas of personality and cognitive development cross-culturally, the evaluation of educational programs, the study of attitudes toward family planning, and the relationship of culture and personality. A great deal of ferment to produce organized research is currently developing at the Faculty of Psychology of the Universidad Nacional Autónoma de México. There is a large amount of ongoing research on child development, concept formation, imitation, academic behavior, language, and schedules of reinforcements. Studies are also being initiated in the areas of physiological psychology, social psychology, behavior modification, and animal experimentation.

Publications

In the last 25 years, a large number of journals of psychology were started, but many of them disappeared after a few issues.

At the present time there are a number that are in the process of being started. The *Revista Mexicana de Investigación Psicológica* is sponsored by the Sociedad Mexicana de Psicología, A.C. The address is Filadélfia 119–202, México 18, D.F. *Enseñanza e Investigación* en Psicología is the journal of the Consejo Nacional para la Enseñanza e Investigación en Psicología. The address is Editor General, Dr. Juán Lafarga, Avenida Cerro de las Torres 395, México 21, D.F.

Occupational Distribution

Ten years ago the largest number of psychologists were engaged in vocational and educational guidance. Even now, many psychologists practice school psychology. Next in number of practitioners at that time was clinical psychology, which is now practiced both in private offices and in clinics and hospitals. A substantial number of psychologists work in the public service. Industrial psychology has a number of representatives also, and teaching of psychology is particularly in demand at the present time because of the large number of students that are enrolling and because of the ever-increasing number of departments of psychology that are being opened in the state universities across the country. Psychologists are also found to be associated with criminologists and other specialists in prisons, and a few are becoming researchers.

Opportunities for Foreign Psychologists

Mexico has kept its doors open for political refugees from any type of dictatorship. In this way, a number of foreign psychologists who were politically persecuted in their own countries have entered Mexico and been given opportunity to work. The laws of Mexico are quite liberal in regard to highly qualified professionals in any branch of knowledge for which there are no representatives in Mexico or no representatives of a high level of technological sophistication. These individuals can be brought to Mexico by different universities or institutions, as long as they dedicate an important part of their time to helping local professional people to acquire their skills.

It is, however, definitely not advisable for any individual psychologist from the United States or any other country to come on his own to try to start private practice or practice in clinics, hospitals, etc. The requirements that must be fulfilled by institutions or groups in Mexico that wish to invite specialists to come to Mexico for short or long periods of time are rather complex, and an individual psychologist trying to make his way by himself into Mexico would probably have 90 chances in 100 of failing. On the other hand, invitations to give seminars or workshops can be easily arranged. Most of the interested groups are either the societies or the departments of psychology within the universities.

Nepal[1]

Education and Training

As of 1976, the system of higher education in Nepal (the birthplace of Buddha, but now strongly influenced by Hinduism) consisted of 1 university and 72 undergraduate institutions. The latter begin instruction at a level equivalent to that of the 11th grade in the United States; psychology is offered as a major in 5 of them. Students are given courses in general, abnormal and personality, experimental, physiological, and social psychology. The textbooks used are (with the exception of social) Nepalese translations of U.S. standard works. For example, Munn's *Psychology* is used extensively for the introductory course, Woodworth and Schlosberg for advanced general, and Brown's *Psychodynamics of Abnormal Behavior* for abnormal and personality. Underwood's *Psychological Research* is relied upon for experimental; the laboratory portion of the course, however, is limited to exercises in human learning (e.g., memory drums) and perception (e.g., Muller-Lyer illusion). Psychometrics and statistics are given as part of experimental. There are no animal research facilities, which possibly accounts for the absence of both a text and a laboratory in the physiological course. For social psychology, the Nepalese depend upon an Indian source.

[1]Based on information supplied by Prof. Ayan Bahadur Shrestha, Nepal, and Prof. Joseph Notterman, Princeton, New Jersey.

No psychological program is offered at the graduate level for either academic or clinical areas of specialization. There are only two psychiatrists in the entire country, or an average of one per 40,000 – 45,000 persons. Both these psychiatrists are affiliated with the hospital in Katmandu. The hospital does not have an outpatient clinic.

Netherlands[1]

Introduction

Scientific psychology in the Netherlands was started with F. C. Donders's reaction-time experiments over 100 years ago. The first Dutch psychological laboratory was established in 1892 by Heymans. Buytendijh, the leader of the so-called Utrecht school, attempted to combine the physiological and psychological approach to human behavior.

Contemporary psychological research in the Netherlands, inspired by Rutten, De Groot, and others, encompasses several areas, among them experimental studies in sensation, perception, psycholinguistics, problem solving, mathematical psychology, and social and developmental issues.

National Organization

The National Association of Dutch Psychologists is called Nederlands Instituut van Psychologen (Netherlands Psychological Association—NIP). Its address is Niclaas Maesstraat 112, Amsterdam, the Netherlands, and the official language is Dutch, although correspondence may be in either English, French, or German.

Internal Structure

The ruling body of the NIP is the executive council (dagelijks bestuur) composed of four members: president

[1]Based on information supplied by A. M. Stuyling de Lange, director, Nederlands Instituut Van Psychologen; and other sources.

(voorzitter), vice-president (vice-voorzitter), secretary (secretaris), and treasurer (penningmeester). In addition, there is the general council (hoofdbestuur) consisting of four executive committee members, three council presidents (raden), and eight NIP division presidents (voorzitter). The executive council is elected by direct elections in the general assembly of the members, on proposal of the general council but with the right—after official announcement of proposal—to the members to bring up other names.

Membership

The total number of members in 1978 was 2,156, divided into five categories, as follows: members—1540, associate (junior)—582, fellows (student)—28, member of honor—1, and extraordinary members (buitengewone)—5.

There are eight divisions, as follows: bedrijfspsychologie (labor and organization), beroeskeuze (vocational guidance), kinder and jeugd (development, children and youth), klinische (clinical), onderwijs (educational and school), psychonomie, sociale gerontologie, and sociale psychologie.

Membership Requirements

General admission requirements for a member are a completed university curriculum and the title of doctorandus (Drs.), or a doctor's degree without writing a thesis.

Major Activities

The NIP deals with social and economic problems such as wages, labor conditions (contracts), professional and ethical problems in relation to government, employers, etc. It also handles scientific problems such as curriculum in the universities for psychologists, and law in relation to the profession and toward other disciplines, such as the medical.

The NIP holds meetings twice a year, in April and

November, as well as conferences on psychological or interdisciplinary items. It also publishes an address book.

Education and Training

There are seven schools: universities (state) at Groningen, Leiden, and Utrecht; universities (private) at Amsterdam (city), Amsterdam (free Protestant), Nijmegen (Catholic), and Tilburg (Catholic). Degrees (diplomas, doctorandus) are all state-controlled. The total number of students is 9,000.

The government supervisory system controls programs, number and quality of teachers, and members of the scientific staffs. The state pays all salaries—directly or indirectly. The scientific status of doctorandus (Drs.) is legally protected and state-controlled.

The influence of the national psychological organization is not based on the law but on the relations with the Ministry of Education and Sciences and on the relation with the National Academic Council (president: a psychologist, former president of the NIP) and the Section Psychology of the National Academic Council in which the seven schools are united.

Legal Status

There is no licensing as in the United States. Anyone who receives a doctoral degree can apply for a job—private or governmental—or may start a private practice. The title of psychologist (psycholoog) is protected and based on the diploma of one of the seven schools mentioned.

The professional ethical code applies only to the members of the NIP.

For jobs on the scientific level, the equivalent of a doctoral degree is necessary. Job prospects, due to current unemployment and the large number of graduates flooding a finite job market, are very poor, and there is also a language problem in doing responsible work. However, written Dutch is easier to understand than spoken.

Research

Each of the seven schools has its research programs; sometimes the same work is done at several places at the same time. Resources consist of the school budgets (subfaculteiten psychologie) and budgets granted by state organization ZWO (for purely scientific research). There are few private research centers, mainly big firms (multinationals) having a department of psychology, working on their own problems; there is little exchange of information.

Publications

De Psycholoog, published monthly (11 times a year), is located at the following address: c/o Nederlands Instituut van Psychologen, Nic. Maesstraat 122, Amsterdam.

Nederlands Tijdschrift voor Psychologie, Noordhollandse Uitgeversmij. N.V., Jan van Galenstraat 335, Amsterdam, Nederlands.

Gedrag, Tijdschrift voor Psychologie, c/o G.P. van Galen, Erasmuslaan 16, Nijmegen, Nederlands.

The total number of psychology books published in the Netherlands is 360 per annum.

Occupational Distribution

The 1,540 regular members of the NIP are employed as university professors; as clinicians in hospitals, social welfare centers, and geriatric institutions; in school systems as guidance counselors and school psychologists; and in industry and government.

The universities train 9,000 psychologists, while there are job opportunities for about 3,000 psychologists.

Opportunities for Foreign Psychologists

Dutch universities welcome visiting professors and researchers. Inquiries should be directed to a particular university.

New Zealand[1]

National Organization

The national psychological organization is the
New Zealand Psychological Society, Inc.
c/o Royal Society
Six Halswell Street
P. O. Box 12367
Wellington, New Zealand
The official languages are English and Esperanto.

Internal Structure

The governing body is a council consisting of president, vice-president, immediate past president, secretary, and no more than 15 nor less than 6 members. Day-to-day affairs are in the hands of an executive secretary, who is in touch with the president by telephone. There are six branches in major centers and six divisions. Council and officers are elected at an annual general meeting. Branches and divisions elect their own officers and council representatives at their annual meetings.

Membership

There are five categories of members: fellows, associates, members, subscribers, and student subscribers.

[1]Based on information supplied by C. J. Adcock, executive secretary, New Zealand Psychological Society, Inc., and other sources.

Divisions

The society has five divisions: clinical, educational, behavioral analysis, experimental, and occupational.

Membership Requirements

Simple membership requires a 4-year honors degree or equivalent. A division concerned with the practice of psychology usually requires postgraduate training as for a 2-year diploma course. Associates must have engaged in work of a psychological nature for not less than 2 years after qualifying for membership and must have made a substantial contribution to the advancement of psychological knowledge by research or organizing to be regarded as a highly competent professional psychologist.

For fellowship, a minimum of 7 years after membership is necessary and a substantial and original contribution to knowledge or practice must have been made.

Major Activities

An annual conference of 4 days' duration is held during the latter part of August.

Education and Training

Six universities in New Zealand offer training in psychology. All offer 3-year courses at the bachelor level, honors or master's courses requiring 4 or 5 years, and Ph.D. courses. There are clinical diploma courses in three universities. The estimated number of students enrolled in each program is as follows: bachelor in arts or science—270, honors and master's—84, Ph.D.—40, clinical diploma—12.

Until recent years, New Zealand was largely dependent upon overseas-trained psychologists to meet its needs, but with current training facilities there is some danger of new graduates having difficulty in finding positions. Foreign-trained applicants with special qualifications are often welcomed, but it should be noted that the education department usually stipulates that psychologists should have had experience in teaching children.

Research

Several government departments have research units but they are only indirectly concerned with psychological research and do not have psychological staff to undertake or direct research. Individuals employed as psychologists can expect to be able to devote about 10% of their time to research; research is often done without support.

Universities have limited funds available for research and may receive grants from government bodies for specific projects, but there is little aid from other sources. All the universities have computer facilities and various forms of equipment are available.

Publications

The New Zealand Psychological Society publishes the *New Zealand Psychologist* twice yearly. It is available through the society.

Opportunities for Foreign Psychologists

New Zealand universities and the New Zealand Council for Educational Research welcome foreign psychologists on a visiting professorship or research assignment basis. Interested psychologists should write to one of the universities or to the

New Zealand Council for Educational Research
22 Brandon Street
Wellington, New Zealand

Nigeria[1]

National Organization

The national association of psychologists in Nigeria is the Nigerian Psychological Society at the following address:

c/o Professor E. A. Yoloye
Faculty of Education
University of Ibadan
Ibadan, Nigeria

The official language is English.

Internal Structure

The governing body of the society, the executive committee, formulates policy for the society and represents the society to the government and other agencies. It appoints committees to discuss issues such as provision, qualification, and setting up branches.

Membership

The Nigerian society has over 150 members, divided into divisions or sections including the university teaching group, teacher education group, child guidance group, and test measurement group. These are interest groups rather than fixed divisions.

[1]Based on information supplied by Prof. E. A. Yoloye, University of Ibadan, Nigeria, on behalf of the Nigerian Psychological Society; and other sources.

Membership Requirements

The membership admission requirements include a university degree in which psychology has been taken as one of the courses of study.

Major Activities

The Nigerian Psychological Society holds annual meetings, usually around April, and organizes special conferences that focus on such problems as psychological guidance of the school child and psychology of work.

Education and Training

There are two institutions, the University of Lagos and the University of Nsukka, which offer psychological training and grant B.A., B.Sc., master's, and doctorate degrees. The average number of students is 20 per degree program.

Research

Research facilities exist in government agencies such as West African Examinations Council, Test Development and Research Office (TEDRO); National Educational Research Center (NERC); Comparative Education Study and Adaptation Center (CESAC) and Ministries of Education; and university departments of psychology, educational foundation, human resources unit, etc.

Publications

The *West African Journal of Educational and Vocational Measurement* is published by the West African Examinations Council, Lagos, Nigeria.

Occupational Distribution

Nigerian psychologists are involved in university teaching, vocational educational guidance, and clinical work.

Opportunities for Foreign Psychologists

Foreign-trained psychologists are welcome to work in this country. There is no formal requirement other than qualification and competence in the given area. Inquiries should be addressed to Nigerian consulates.

Norway[1]

National Organization

The national psychological organization in Norway is the
      Norsk Psykologforening (Norwegian
      Psychological Association)
      Bjørn Farmannsgate 16
      Oslo 2, Norway
The official language is Norwegian.

Internal Structure

The association is organized in a general assembly, open
for all members, that meets every 2 years; a council, consisting
of representatives from the local associations; and the central
executive committee, which carries out the policies set by the
general assembly. The executive committee consists of the
president of the association, a vice-president, the chairmen of
the wage committee, educational committee, professional
committee, and public relations committee, and the editor of
the association's journal.

In addition, there is an ethics committee, a research and
test committee, and an election committee. There are 12 local
associations covering the country.

Members of the central executive committee are elected
by the general assembly. Officers to the council are elected by

---

[1]Based on information supplied by the central executive committee of Norsk
Psykologenforening, and other sources.

172

the general assembly of the local associations. Members of the permanent committees are elected by the general assembly.

Membership

There are over 700 members, all of whom belong to the only category of full membership. The local associations have largely replaced earlier divisions. The section of school psychology is still active.

Membership Requirements

To be admitted to membership, one must possess a candidate degree in psychology (Cand. Psychol.) or an equivalent degree.

Major Activities

Annual meetings are held in connection with the general assembly, and Scandinavian congresses in psychology are arranged by the five Scandinavian associations every 3 years.

The association has the responsibility for three professional examining boards (clinical, counseling, and psychotherapy), which grant specialist status in these areas. It also arranges qualifying courses and seminars. The local associations also arrange a variety of seminars every year, alone or in cooperation with the universities.

Education and Training

Four universities, the College of Civil Economics, and the College of Physical Education offer training in psychology.

Two universities, the University of Oslo and the University of Bergen, grant professional degrees in psychology, based on 7 years of university studies (Cand. Psychol.). These two universities and the University of Trondheim also grant a research degree in psychology based on 7 years of university studies

(Mag. Art.). Four universities offer a doctorate of philosophy, which usually is granted after several years of postgraduate research. This degree has no importance for professional practice. Two additional institutions of higher education offer courses in psychology but grant no degree. In addition, many professional schools offer psychology as part of their curriculum.

Legal Status

A licensing law for psychologists was passed by the Norwegian Parliament on March 9, 1973. Only those who have a professional degree and have served an internship in psychology as required by the statutes can use the title of psychologist. License can also be granted if equivalent education and professional skills in psychology can be documented.

A code of professional ethics is regulated by law. Violation of the code can result in penalty and loss of license. The national association regulates the professional conduct of its members through a detailed ethical code and through its board of professional ethics.

Research

There are governmental research institutions for applied social research, geriatric psychology, occupational psychology, alcohol research, and military psychology, all of which employ research psychologists.

There are six institutes of psychology in universities and schools of higher education, all of which carry out research in psychology. Basic research is conducted within most fields. Lately, applied psychological research has been given much attention in the universities. Well-equipped laboratories exist in most institutes.

Psychological research is carried out in several psychiatric institutions, hospitals and health institutions, educational institutions, vocational rehabilitation centers, etc.

The Norwegian Research Council for the Sciences and

Humanities annually gives grants for research in psychology. During the last years about 50 to 60 research projects have received annual grants from the council in addition to the grants given by the universities and other governmental funding agencies.

Publications

The following psychological journals are published in Norway:

Tidsskrift for Norsk Psykologforening (Journal of the Norwegian Psychological Association), Bjørn Framannsgate 16, Oslo 2; 12 issues annually.

Skolepsykologi (Journal of School Psychology), Boks 121, 2760 Brandbu; 6 issues annually.

Nordisk Psykologi (Journal of Nordic Psychology), Akademisk Forlag, St. Kannikestraede 6−8, 1169 København K, Denmark; 4 issues annually.

Journal of Scandinavian Psychology, c/o Lars Kebbon, Ullerakers sjukhus, S-750 17, Uppsala, Sweden; 4 issues annually.

University of Oslo publication series in psychology, Psykologist Instituut, Boks 1094, Blindern, Oslo 3.

University of Bergen publication series in psychology, Psykologisk Instituut, Universitetet, 500 Bergen.

Journal of Social Research, Instituut for samfunnsforskning, Munthesgate 31, Oslo 2.

Impuls, Psykologist Instituut, Boks 1094, Blindern, Oslo 3.

Elektra, Psykologisk Instituut, Universitetet, 5000 Bergen.

Fokus på familien, Boks 60, 3371 Vikersund.

Tidsskrift for miljøterapi, c/o Arild Jørgensen, 3371 Vikersund.

Occupational Distribution

Norwegian psychologists work in a variety of fields. Over 250 occupy teaching and research positions in universities and schools of higher learning. Over 350 work in the clinical field in hospitals and clinics, and some of them are in private practice. Over 200 psychologists work in the school system as school psychologists and guidance counselors. Some psychologists work in industry and government.

Opportunities for Foreign Psychologists

Foreign-trained psychologists can gain professional employment if they satisfy the requirements set by the licensing law for psychologists. The governmental psychology board evaluates each applicant.

Inquiries should be addressed to the Norwegian consulates.

Pakistan[1]

National Organization

The national organization is the Pakistan Psychological Association. There is no permanent office of the organization, but at present the central office is located in the Department of Psychology, University of Peshawar, Peshawar, Pakistan. The official languages are English and Urdu.

Internal Structure

The association consists of the general body and the executive committee. The executive committee is composed of the president, the president-elect, a vice-president, a general secretary, two assistant secretaries, a treasurer, and four other members. The executive committee is elected by the general body.

Membership

At present there are 250 general members. In order to be a member a person must be a Pakistani national and have at least a master's or a B.A. honors degree in psychology and must be academically or professionally associated with the subject. Scholars from allied disciplines are eligible for associate membership, and foreign psychologists may be enrolled as foreign affiliates.

[1]Based on information supplied by Prof. S. M. Poghni, president, Pakistan Psychological Association, and other sources.

The association was formed in 1968 in Dacca at the first annual conference of the association. Due to subsequent political turmoil in the country, which finally resulted in the breakup of Pakistan, the activities of the association came to a halt. Recently, efforts have been made to revive the association, and the second annual meeting was held in 1976.

Education and Training

The educational structure in Pakistan is such that each student must have 10 years of schooling before he enters a college for a 2-year intermediate education. After passing the intermediate examination, he may enter a college for a B.A./B.Sc. degree (2 years) or a university for a B.A./S.Sc. honors (3 years) course. This finally leads to an M.A./M.Sc. in psychology, which is of 2 years' duration for B.A./B.Sc. holders, and 1 year's duration for B.A./B.Sc. honors degree holders.

Courses in introductory psychology are available to the students of both arts and science, at intermediate level and onward. Most colleges in Pakistan offer courses in psychology and it is quite a popular subject at this level. Out of six universities, four have postgraduate departments in psychology. The governmental college in Lahore also has a postgraduate department in psychology; thus, there are five postgraduate departments that offer courses leading to an M.A./M.Sc. in psychology (or applied psychology, in the case of Punjab University). Some universities also grant the degrees of M.Phil. and Ph.D.

Research

The research work in Pakistan is still rather elementary, due to paucity of funds and personnel. Some studies conducted in the United States and the United Kingdom have been replicated. An effort has been made to translate tests into Urdu (the national language of Pakistan) and to standardize them on a Pakistani sample. DAT, MMPI, and some other tests of achievement and intelligence have been translated and adopted. Some social psychological research on problems of stereotypes and social distance has also been done.

Publications

There is no journal owned by the Pakistan Psychological Association. However, a number of journals are published. *Pakistan Journal of Psychology* (University of Karachi) has been appearing regularly for the last 10 years. Other journals are *Pakistan Psychological Studies* (Department of Psychology of the University of Peshawar) and *Psychology Quarterly* (Government College of Lahore); these have been appearing rather irregularly. Government College of Lahore also publishes an Urdu periodical, *Shaoor,* for lay readers. Recently, *Psychologists' Newsletter* has appeared, which publishes news and other articles of professional interest for psychologists.

Other outlets of research articles are *Pakistan Journal of Philosophy* (published by the Pakistan Philosophical Congress) and *Journal of Scientific Research* (Punjab University, Lahore).

The books published in Pakistan are either translations of foreign textbooks or textbooks written in Urdu for intermediate and B.A./B.Sc. levels.

Occupational Distribution

Most of the psychologists are at present employed in the teaching profession, although a few are working as clinical psychologists in hospitals. The armed forces, the public service commission, and the government departments of education also employ a few psychologists for selection of personnel and research work.

Opportunities for Foreign Psychologists

Foreign psychologists interested in visiting or permanent occupation in Pakistan must contact Pakistani consulates.

Panama[1]

National Organization

The national psychological organization is the
Asociación Panameña de Psicólogos
P.O. Box 6-415-E1 Dorado, Panamá
Republic of Panama
The official language is Spanish.

Internal Structure

Members of the board are president, vice-president, secretary, undersecretary, treasurer, three directors, and an advisory council (formed by all former presidents), elected for 1-year periods.

Membership

The association has 90 members, divided into three categories: titular—85, associate—4, and affiliate—1.

Sections. Section I, clinical and counseling psychology, has 10 members; Section II, therapeutic psychology, 18 members; Section III, educational psychology and special education, 10 members; Section IV, social and industrial psychology, 8 members; Section V, psychology of scientific communications, 8 members; and Section VI, psychology of experimental analysis of behavior, 9 members.

[1]Based on information supplied by Prof. Pablo Antonio Thalassinos, president, Asociación Panameña de Psicólogos, and other sources.

Membership Requirements

To be admitted to membership in the association, one must hold a licenciatura degree in psychology, must present an original research paper, and must be proposed by two titular members. Those who hold a graduate degree in psychology but lack the basic licenciatura degree in psychology are classified as associates. Foreigners can become classified as affiliate members.

Major Activities

The association holds a convention once a year. Special conferences of specific orientation are held yearly—e.g., symposia of behavior modification, psychoanalysis, Rogerian theories, transactional analysis.

The association also sponsors conferences in schools, hospitals, and guidance centers.

Education and Training

Two schools offer degrees in psychology: the University of Panama and the Catholic Santa María La Antigua University. The degree offered is licenciatura, a 5-year program at about the master's level. Accreditation is granted by the Ministry of Education. Private schools must follow the programs of the national university.

Legal Status

Panama did not have psychology certified until September 16, 1975. The association worked together with the national government to obtain a law that certifies psychology. To receive the certification, the person should have the basic licenciatura degree. In order to be in private practice or to work in any specialty of the profession, the psychologist must hold a specialized degree.

The association has a professional ethical code and an elected (every 2 years) committee of professional ethics.

Research

Research is conducted at the hospitals. No grants are available, but the research expenses are usually covered by the hospitals.

Publications

Redepsi, Journal of Psychology, P.O. Box 944, Panama 9-A, Panama, is a semiannual publication; the editor is Pablo Thalassinos.

Archivos Panameños de Psicología is an annual publication; the editor is Dr. Ramon de Aguilar, Panama, Panama.

Occupational Distribution

Panama's psychologists occupy academic priorities and are employed in the educational and mental health systems.

Opportunities for Foreign Psychologists

Foreign-trained psychologists, according to the law that certifies psychology in the Republic of Panama, should have their degree revalidated at the University of Panama before applying for the certification that enables them to practice in Panama. Inquiries should be directed to one of the two universities.

Paraguay[1]

National Organization

In 1975 Paraguay's psychologists formed their national organization. Its name and address are as follows:

Sociedad Paraguaya de Psicología
Eduardo V. Haedo 535
Asunción, Paraguay

The official language is Spanish.

Internal Structure

The ruling body is the comision directive. The sociedad has about 100 members divided into three categories: (1) honorary members—psychologists who substantially contributed to the development of scientific psychology in Paraguay; (2) active members—psychologists who hold proper degrees in psychology; and (3) student members.

The sociedad is in the process of forming four divisions: (1) clinical, (2) labor issues, (3) social, and (4) educational.

Major Activities

The sociedad holds general membership meetings twice a year.

---

[1]Based on information supplied by Carlos Luis La Fuenta Glecha, on behalf of the Sociedad Paraguaya de Psicología; and other sources.

Education and Training

The Catholic University (Universidad Católica Nuestra Señora de la Asunción) was the first to establish a psychology department and laboratory. At the present time, three universities in Paraguay offer training in psychology; all three grant the degree of licenciado in psicología, one grants doctorates and one the postgraduate title of clinical psychologist. About 30 students are enrolled in these programs.

Occupational Distribution

Psychologists in Paraguay work in three main areas, namely, as university teachers, in the school system as school psychologists, as guidance and vocational counselors, and as clinical psychologists in hospitals and private practice. A few work in industry.

Opportunities for Foreign Psychologists

Foreign psychologists (who speak Spanish) who are interested in permanent or visiting positions in Paraguay should contact the universities in Paraguay.

Peru[1]

National Organization

The national association of psychologists in Peru was formed in 1954. Its name and address are as follows:

Sociedad Peruana de Psicología
Avenida Larco 656, 2° Piso 2-C
Miraflores, Lima, Perú
Apartado 12520, Lima 21

The official language is Spanish.

Internal Structure

The governing bodies of the sociedad are (1) the general assembly of active members and (2) the executive council (la junta directiva) consisting of president, vice-president, secretary general, treasurer, and secretaries of special areas. The junta is elected for 2 years.

The main aims of the sociedad are to promote scientific activities in psychology and to represent the professional psychologists.

Membership

The total number of members is over 400. They are divided into four categories: (1) active members, who must hold

[1]Based on information supplied by Reynaldo Alarcón, president, Sociedad Peruana de Psicología, and other sources.

185

the title Psicólogo or licenciado en psicología issued by a recognized Peruvian or foreign university; (2) affiliate members, who must have a B.A. degree; (3) honorary members, who have made an outstanding contribution to psychology; (4) corresponding members—foreign psychologists.

The sociedad does not have distinct divisions, but it has special secretaries who organize conferences of clinical, educational, industrial, and social psychologists.

Major Activities

The sociedad takes an active part in planning psychological training programs at the various universities. The sociedad organizes symposia and conferences, and in December 1975 it held the First Peruvian Congress of Psychology with the participation of 1,800 people.

Education and Training

All 30 universities in Peru teach psychology. The following 9 universities offer full programs leading to the degree of bachiller en psicología and the professional titles of psicólogo and licenciado en psicología: Universidad Nacional Mayor de San Marcos, Universidad Católica del Perú, Universidad Nacional Federico Villareal, Universidad Inca Garcilaso de la Vega, Universidad Femenina, Universidad San Martín de Porres, Universidad Cayetano Heredia, Universidad Ricardo Palma, and Universidad San Agustín.

The first eight universities are in Lima, the last one is in Arequipa.

Peruvian universities operate on a "credits" system, similar to universities in the United States. The bachelor degree is based on 132 credits; the psychologist degree is based on 198 credits, 1 year of internship, a thesis in the field of applied psychology, and proper examinations.

The university curricula and the level of instruction and the granting of degrees are supervised by El Consejo Nacional de la Universidad Peruana (CONUP), National Council of Peruvian Universities.

Research

Psychological research in Peru is primarily empirical, quantitative, and experimental, partially related to problems of applied psychology. Psychometrics, standardization of intelligence, personality, and vocational tests are some of the major research areas. Research in developmental psychology is influenced by Piaget's theories, and sociopsychological studies are much concerned with the changing social climate and intergroup relations in Peru.

Research centers at the universities support basic and applied studies.

The Instituto Nacional de Investigaciones Educacionales (INIDE) (the National Institute for Educational Research) of the Peruvian Ministry of Public Education supports research in social psychology. Several private institutes support anthropological, industrial, and clinical studies.

Publications

The Sociedad Peruvana de Psicología publishes an informative bulletin. Some universities publish various reports, bulletins, and periodicals.

Occupational Distribution

Peruvian psychologists work in a variety of fields of academic and applied psychology. They are employed as university professors, as school psychologists and guidance counselors for the school system, as clinical psychologists in hospitals and private practice, and as industrial and social psychologists by governmental and private agencies.

Opportunities for Foreign Psychologists

Peruvian universities welcome visiting professors and researchers. Inquiries should be addressed to a particular university.

Philippines[1]

National Organization

In 1962 psychologists in the Philippines formed their national organization,

> Psychological Association of the Philippines (PAP)
> Psychology Department/C.A.S.
> University of the Philippines
> Quezon City 3004
> Philippines

The official languages are English and Pilipino.

Internal Structure

A board of directors is the governing body of the association. The aims of the association are (1) to advance learning, teaching, and research in psychology as a science; (2) to promote human welfare; and (3) to advance the practice of psychology as an independent, scientifically oriented, and ethically conscious profession.

Membership

The bylaws of the association distinguish four categories of members:

Fellows. These shall be individuals whose occupation and activities are primarily in the advancement of psychology

[1]Based on information supplied by Dr. Natividad Munarriz, president, Psychological Association of the Philippines, and other sources.

as a science and as a profession, and who shall satisfy the following minimum standards: (1) a doctoral degree in psychology proper, or in any of its major subdivisions, which is based in part on a scientific dissertation of acceptable standard on a problem in psychology and which is conferred by a graduate school of recognized standing; and (2) previous membership as an associate with published psychological researches of acceptable standards.

Associates. These shall be individuals whose occupation and activities are primarily in the advancement of psychology as a science and as a profession. They must have (1) finished an M.A. degree in psychology proper, or any of its major subdivisions, which is based in part on a scientific dissertation of acceptable standards on a problem in psychology and which is conferred by a graduate school of recognized standing; or (2) finished a bachelor's degree in psychology and have had at least 5 years of acceptable professional experience subsequent to the granting of the bachelor's degree.

Affiliate Members. Individuals with the following qualifications may become affiliates: (1) graduate or undergraduate students majoring in psychology; (2) psychologists who are nonpermanent residents of the Philippines or psychologists of foreign countries and members of a bonafide psychological association of their respective countries; (3) Specialists in related fields who are interested in psychology and who have done studies that have contributed to its development.

Major Activities

Major activities are an annual convention (2 or 3 days), which features a symposium, research papers, and ensuing open forums.

In 1973–1974 a special meeting was held by the board members with chairmen of departments of psychology of some 10 institutions of higher learning in the greater Manila area to discuss problems in the teaching of psychology (a required subject in many academic programs). As a result of this meeting, the PAP organized a seminar on the teaching of psychology, which was offered in conjunction with the Department of Psychology of the Ateneo de Manila University.

Currently, activities are planned for more active participation of the membership.

Education and Training

All universities in the Philippines offer psychology programs, and some offer B.A., M.A., and Ph.D. degrees similar to those from universities in the United States.

Publications

The PAP publishes a journal, *Philippine Journal of Psychology,* twice a year.

Opportunities for Foreign Psychologists

Foreign psychologists wishing to settle or to obtain a visiting position in the Philippines should consult consular services or write directly to one of the universities in the Philippines.

Poland[1]

Introduction

The first university to introduce psychology was the University of Lwów in 1876 (at that time Lwów was part of Austria). The first psychological laboratory was opened in 1901 at that university by Kazimierz Twardowski, Brentano's disciple. The second psychological laboratory, clearly experimental, was established in 1903 by Wladyslaw Heinrich at the Jagiello University in Cracow, and the third at the University of Warsaw by Edward Abramowski.

For decades Polish psychology was under West European influence, mostly German and French. Since World War II the Russian influence has prevailed, with some emphasis on Marxian philosophy and Pavlov's neuropsychology. At present, Polish universities remain open to Russian, West European, and American influences, and to all aspects of contemporary psychological research and theory.

National Organization

In 1949 the Polish Psychological Association (PTP) was formed. Its address is:

Polskie Towarzystwo Psychologiczne (PTP)
Stawki 5/7, 00-183
Warsaw, Poland

The official language is Polish.

[1]Based on information supplied by J. Bierzwińska, magister filosofii, secretary general of the Polish Psychological Association, and other sources.

192

Internal Structure

The general assembly, meeting once a year, elects the central board every 3 years and approves the central council's annual reports.

The central council convokes the general assembly, reports annually on its own work and the work of PTP branches, puts the general assembly's resolutions into effect, pursues the goals of the PTP as defined in its statutes, contacts the respective government, municipal, and scientific institutions on matters affecting PTP, supervises the work of PTP branches, aiding them in organizational and scientific matters, and supervises publishing and other activities.

The court of conciliation investigates cases of dispute and violations of the code of ethics, etc.

The general assembly elects (by secret ballot) the central council, the auditing commission, and the court of conciliation. The branch executives and the auditing commissions of the branches are elected at general assemblies of members in the given area.

Membership

About 1,000 psychologists belong to the PTP. There are three categories of membership: members—865, associate members—128, and honorary members—7.

The membership of the Polish Psychological Association has five sections: (1) educational psychology, (2) clinical psychology, (3) labor psychology, (4) vocational counseling, and (5) rehabilitation.

Membership in each section varies from time to time.

Membership Requirements

Any university graduate of psychology may become a member. Other professionals may become associate members upon recommendation of two PTP members.

Major Activities

The annual general assembly of PTP members is held in the autumn (September–October) and is attended by delegates from the various branches.

National scientific congresses are usually held every 3 years. Each section holds its scientific meetings, symposia, and conferences, some with the participation of foreign scientists.

Periodic advancement courses for specialists, publication activities, and methodological work are among the activities of the association.

Education and Training

Eight schools of higher learning, including seven institutes at state universities and one faculty at the Catholic University of Lublin, offer training in psychology. All these schools offer two kinds of degrees: magister (M.A.) in psychology and doctor (Ph.D.) in psychology. Every year some 400–450 magister degrees and some 50–60 doctorates are granted.

A uniform curriculum of psychology courses has been laid down by the Ministry of Science and Higher Education and Technology. The curriculum specifies all obligatory subjects and how to implement them (e.g., through lectures, seminars, practicals), as well as the subjects for each specialization, and all the examinations and other requirements.

The PTP takes part in conferences at which the curriculum of psychology studies is drafted and the organization and streamlining of courses are discussed.

Practically all schools in psychology and all current trends are represented in Polish universities' advanced programs in psychology. In addition to psychological theories and experimental psychology, Polish universities offer advanced training in clinical, educational, and social psychology.

Legal Status

No further requirements exist beyond those implemented within the university courses. Upon obtaining his M.A., the psychology graduate is entitled to assume the post of psychologist.

There is no private practice for psychologists in Poland. The PTP has laid down the Psychologist's Code of Ethics, which specifies the recommendations for and standards to be met by psychologists at work. The code was published in English in the *Polish Psychological Bulletin*, 1974, 5, 107–109.

Research

Research work is subsidized by the government and conducted under the supervision of the Polish Academy of Sciences. Grants may be obtained by persons or institutions upon submission of suitable research projects. The universities of Warsaw, Cracow, and Poznan conduct extensive and diversified research. The universities are supported by the Ministry of Science and Higher Education and Technology and may use their resources to subsidize research projects.

Publications

The following journals are published in Poland in connection with psychology:

Przegląd Psychologiczny (Psychological Review), the organ of the PTP, a quarterly; address: Al. Stalingradzka 1, 61–712 Poznan, Poland.

Polish Psychological Bulletin, published quarterly in English by the Polish Academy of Sciences, cosponsored by the PTP; address: Stawki 5/7, 00-183 Warsaw, Poland.

Studia Psychologiczne, an annual publication of the Polish Academy of Sciences; address: Stawki 5-7, 00-183 Warsaw, Poland.

Poland annually publishes from 100 to 200 books on psychology.

Occupational Distribution

About 600 Polish psychologists teach at the universities. About 1,000 work in the educational system as school psychologists and guidance counselors. Approximately 800 engage in clinical work in hospitals and other mental health centers but none are in private practice. About 1,700 work for governmental agencies in industry, legal systems, etc.

Opportunities for Foreign Psychologists

Psychologists who seek permanent or prolonged employment in Poland should contact a Polish consulate. As a rule, persons who hold a degree granted by a foreign school and who are not Polish citizens are required to notarize it and obtain the permission of the police authorities, the application for which is made by the prospective employer.

The detailed notarization procedures vary with the country of origin, being subject to intergovernmental agreements.

Psychologists who wish to work in Poland on a temporary basis as visiting professors or researchers should contact one of the Polish universities.

Portugal[1]

National Organization

The name and address of the Portuguese Society for Psychology are as follows:

> Sociedade Portuguesa de Psicologia
> Avenida Magalhaes Lima, 6-1°-D
> Lisboa 1
> Portugal

The official language is Portuguese.

Membership Requirements

One must possess a high degree in psychology to be admitted to full membership of the sociedade.

Education and Training

The universities of Coimbra, Lisbon, Louenco, Luanda, and Porto offer courses in psychology. Advanced training is given at the Coimbra and Lisbon universities with an emphasis on educational and clinical psychology. These two universities award the postgraduate degree of licentiate in psychology.

The Centro de Psicologia Aplicado and the Instituto de Orientaco Professional, both at the Lisbon university, offer advanced training in vocational guidance, counseling, testing and measurement, and diagnostic methods.

[1]Based on information supplied by various sources.

Several Portuguese psychologists receive postgraduate training in psychoanalysis and other therapeutic methods under the auspices of the Portuguese Society of Neurology and Psychiatry.

Legal Status

Holders of the licentiate or doctorate in psychology are recognized as psychologists. The civil service examination entitles psychologists to practice psychology in clinical, industrial, and educational settings.

Research and Publications

Portuguese psychologists take part in clinical psychoanalytic and neuropathological research. Some of their works are published in Brazil.

Opportunities for Foreign Psychologists

Foreign psychologists interested in temporary or long-term occupation in Portugal should write to the
Secretaria-General
Ministerio de Educação Nacional
Centro de Informação e Relaçóes Públicas Cireo
Avenida Miguel Bombarda, 20 B
Lisboa 1, Portugal

Qatar[1]

National Organization

No national organization exists in the country.

Educational Facilities

Psychology is taught at the Teachers' Training Institute and at the Faculties of Education, which were founded only 3 years ago. The address is:

Faculties of Education
P. O. Box 2713
Doha, State of Qatar
Arabian Gulf

No degree in psychology is offered at present. Students in the Faculty of Education are required to take 18 credits of psychology as part of the requirement for a B.A. degree. At the institute only a few courses are offered.

Approximately 150 men and 200 women are involved at the Faculty of Education degree program.

Research

Any research that is being done is centered at the Faculty of Education, which cooperates with government agencies when called upon. Research is primarily of an applied nature

[1]Based on information supplied by Mohamed Kazem, professor and dean, Faculties of Education, Doha-Qatar, and other sources.

and related to development projects in the country. One example of this type is a survey of intelligence of all 1st-year elementary-school boys in the country in cooperation with the student health service. All research is funded by the college.

Occupational Distribution

So far, the main occupation of psychologists has been teaching at the Faculty of Education, which is above the national average for professional jobs. The language of instruction is Arabic.

Opportunities for Foreign Psychologists

Psychologists interested in temporary or permanent teaching jobs should contact the consuls of the State of Qatar.

Romania[1]

National Organization

The national organization in Romania is the Romanian Psychological Association.

Asociatia Psihologilor din Republica Socialista Romania
Str. Frumoasa nr. 26
sector 8 - Bucharest
Romania

The official language is Romanian.

Internal Structure

Management of the association is in the hands of a general assembly, which elects the association bureau, approves the modification of the association's rules, decides about receiving or excluding members, and approves the association action plan. The association's bureau consists of specialists from different psychological fields and has the following duties: It conducts the association's activity between assemblies, prepares the association's plans of action, and keeps contact with state authorities and with scientific institutions in Romania and abroad. The association's bureau is elected by open vote by the general assembly for a period of 2 years.

[1]Based on information supplied by Constantin Voicu, secretary-general of the Association of Psychology in Romania, and other sources.

Membership

The association has about 500 members, who are divided into the following sections, according to the members' professional interests: (1) work psychology section, (2) educational psychology section, (3) clinical and medical psychology section, (4) physical training and sport commission, (5) suggestion and hypnosis section, (6) national commission of tests.

The association has branches in the more important towns of the country: Bucharest, Cluj, Napoca, and Jassy.

Membership Requirements

Any person who has graduated in psychology, carries on a scientific, didactic, or practical activity in psychology, and has a recommendation from two association members may become a member of the association.

Major Activities

General assemblies or plenary meetings are assigned to some topics of general interest for all psychologists in Romania.

National conferences on psychology, some of them with international participation, as well as thematic symposia for the members of the association are also organized.

Education and Training

All students who are matriculated in institutes of higher education and sections of psychology at the universities of Bucharest, Cluj, Napoca, and Jassy receive full training in psychology. The degrees conferred are called university diplomate—specialty in psychology. The number of students that may be admitted at entrance examination in psychology sections of the university is established by the state plan, depending on the requests of high schools, on the demands of research, and on other practical considerations. After graduating and passing the state examination, the young psychologists are placed by a governmental commission in different jobs in industrial enterprises, hospitals, schools, and research institutes.

The conclusions and recommendations of researchers in pedagogical psychology, including those that result from the debates organized in collaboration with the section of psychology and pedagogy of the Academy of Social and Political Sciences, are communicated to the Ministry of Education and Instruction in order to support a scientific basis for the organization of an educational system and improvement of teaching methods in schools.

University studies in psychology last 4 years. At the section of psychology at the universities of Bucharest, Cluj, and Jassy the following subjects, among other things, are taught: general psychology, child psychology, educational psychology, work psychology, social psychology, psychopathology, clinical psychology, experimental psychology, psychodiagnosis, psychophysiology, psychology of sensory and mental deficiencies, statistics, history of psychology, and foreign languages (English, French, Russian). The students also participate in practice teaching in schools, and receive practical training in laboratories of applied psychology and research institutes.

After graduating, students have to pass a state examination and submit a diploma paper.

Holders of university diplomas in psychology, after 3 years of practice, may apply for doctor's degrees. After passing the examinations and acceptance of their doctoral thesis, they may receive the doctor's degree in psychology. Only the universities of Bucharest, Cluj, Napoca, and Jassy have the right to grant the title of doctor in psychology.

The Romanian Psychological Association debated and approved the "deontologic norms of practicians-psychologists." These principles have been published in *Revista de Psihologie*, 1975, No. 2, 221.

Research

Research in psychological fields is conducted in research institutes, centers, and laboratories of psychology, in departments of psychology at the universities of Bucharest, Cluj, Napoca, and Jassy, and in laboratories of psychology in hospitals, industrial enterprises, schools, etc.

The most important research in psychological fields is carried on in the Institute of Pedagogical and Psychological Research of the Ministry of Education and Instruction, with the Institute of Psychology of the Academy of Social and Political Sciences.

Within the Institute of Pedagogical and Psychological Research, various research projects in different fields of psychology are carried on, including educational psychology, work (industrial) psychology, social psychology, general psychology, psychophysiology, art psychology, sport psychology, and psychology of personality.

Psychological research depends on contracts between the Ministry of Education or the Academy of Social and Political Sciences and industrial enterprises, cultural institutions, and institutions of art. The Institute of Pedagogical and Psychological research has its own research laboratories with modern equipment. Some research projects that have an interdisciplinary character are carried on in collaboration with pedagogues, engineers, physicians, and other specialists.

There are psychological laboratories in other research institutes also, among them the Institute of Technical Research—Railway; the Institute of Scientific Research for Work Protection; the Institute of Energy Research and Modernization; the Center for Research of the Ministry of Chemistry; the Center for Didactic Staff Improvement; the Institute of Neurology and Psychiatry of the Academy of Medical Sciences; the Institute of Geriatrics; and the Institute of Hygiene.

There are psychology laboratories at all great enterprises and industrial centers: Psychology Laboratories of the Ministry of Transport and Telecommunications; Psychology Laboratories of the Ministry of Electric Energy; Laboratories of Transport Enterprise—Bucharest; Psychology Laboratories of Ministry of Metalurgy—Resita, Galati, Hunedoara; Psychology Laboratories of Chemical Enterprise—Fagaras; Psychology

Laboratory of the Enterprise of Radio Pieces and Semiconductors—Baneasa; Psychology Laboratories of the Ministry of Armed Forces, etc.

Publications

The results of psychological research are published in *Revista de Psihologie* (set up in 1955, four issues per year) and in a foreign-language review (English, French, Russian, German), *Revue Roumaine des Sciences Sociales, Série de Psychologie* (set up in 1964, two numbers per year). Both journals are published by the Academy of Social and Political Sciences of the Socialist Republic of Romania.

The publishing house of the Academy of Social and Political Sciences of the Socialist Republic of Romania, the Didactic and Pedagogic Publishing House, and the publishing house of the Ministry of Education publish Romanian scholarly works in psychology.

Occupational Distribution

Most Romanian psychologists occupy teaching positions in the nation's 50 schools of higher learning and in governmental agencies as related to organizational and industrial psychology. There is no private clinical practice and Romania's clinical psychologists work in governmental hospitals and clinics. Schools are another area of employment for psychologists, and a great many Romanian psychologists are involved in the school system as psychologists and guidance workers.

Opportunities for Foreign Psychologists

Foreign psychologists wishing to conduct research or be appointed visiting professors must apply to Romania's consulates.

Singapore[1]

National Organization

There is as yet no official national psychological organization in Singapore. Various attempts have been made by psychologists in the past few years to form such an organization or society.

Educational Facilities

There is no department of psychology in the two universities (University of Singapore and Nanyang University) in Singapore.

Psychology is taught only as a subsidiary subject in several university departments, (e.g., social work, sociology, business administration) at the Institute of Education and School of Nursing.

Legal Status

A person with a recognized honors degree (e.g., B.A., Hons.) or equivalent may apply for a post of psychologist. However, preference is given to persons with relevant postgraduate qualifications in psychology. The Public Service Commission is the appointing authority. There is no professional code of ethics for psychologists. Psychologists in government service are subject to all the rules and regulations laid

[1]Based on information supplied by Raymond H. T. Wong, the Permanent Mission of Singapore to the United Nations, and other sources.

down in the instruction manual and general orders for all civil servants.

Research and Publications

Any psychological research is done on an individual basis. There is no large-scale psychological research project involving government agencies or research centers.

There is no national psychological journal in Singapore. Psychologists in Singapore submit articles to overseas psychological journals or to the local *Singapore Medical Journal* (address: Singapore Medical Association, 4A College Road, Singapore 3).

Occupational Distribution

Nine Singapore psychologists work in hospitals, seven in research, four in vocational guidance, three in the Institute of Education, and three in management.

Opportunities for Foreign Psychologists

Foreign psychologists interested in temporary or permanent jobs in Singapore should contact Singapore diplomatic posts.

South Africa[1]

National Organizations

The South African Psychological Association (SAPA) is the main national organization. There is also an organization serving primarily Afrikaans-speaking psychologists, i.e., the Psychological Institute of the Republic of South Africa, but SAPA is the internationally affiliated and recognized association. Its address is:

P. O. Box 4292
Johannesburg 2000
South Africa

The official languages are English and Afrikaans.

Internal Structure

Office-bearers in the association form the council, which is responsible for all affairs of the association. The executive committee of the council is composed of those members of Council present in the Johannesburg area. This body effectively runs the day-to-day affairs of the association (monthly meetings) through the secretariat. Standing executive committees deal with special aspects such as publications, professional affairs, and special-interest groups.

The president of the association is elected by the council. Since branches contribute two members each to the council

[1]Based on information supplied by Prof. R. D. Griesel, secretary-general of the South African Psychological Association, and other sources.

and further make nominations at the time of such elections, members have an indirect voice in the election of the president. Three vice-presidents are nominated by individual members and elected at the annual general meeting. At the same meeting, after the same nomination procedure, three further members of the council and a secretary are elected.

Membership

Total membership of the SAPA is approximately 400, with an approximate division as follows: full members—130, associate members—210, student members—40, emeritus members—2, honorary members—18.

The association has no divisions or sections according to interest groups.

Membership Requirements

Full members are required to have at least a master's degree in psychology; associate members, at least 1 year of university study in psychology. Student members should be full-time registered university students of psychology who do not yet have an honors B.A. Emeritus members are previously full members who have retired from full-time employment as psychologists, and honorary members are persons elected by the council by virtue of their services to the association or some other outstanding contribution to psychology as a profession.

Major Activities

Annual meetings are usually held in July each year in various centers in the republic, usually every alternate year in Johannesburg. Most of the association's activities occur at branch level. The branches meet four to eight times per year, offering a variety of activities.

The second national organization of South African psychologists is the Psychological Institute of the Republic of South Africa (PIRSA).

Education and Training

Approximately 18 universities and/or university colleges offer academic training, and 5 universities offer practical post-graduate training. Of the 18 universities, all except 6 that can offer only up to the master's level offer degrees up to and including doctorates. The number of students in each degree or diploma course varies greatly with the size of the university but decreases with advanced courses. First-year classes may be as large as 1,000 but there are relatively few doctoral students. Of the approximate 120,000 students in the country, about 7,000 are at 1st-year level, 4,000 2nd-year, 2,000 final-year bachelor's, 500 honors bachelor's, 200 master's, and 100 doctorate in psychology, i.e., some 13,800 total for psychology.

The Professional Board for Psychology considers applications by university psychology departments and other training institutions for accreditation of their training programs. Certain basic minimum standards must be maintained in order that accreditation be obtained.

The South African Psychological Association influences the educational system only indirectly insofar as many of the persons concerned with university and other training who are members of the South African universities, are particularly aware of their role, and guard against intrusion on their autonomy.

Legal Status

There is a statutory obligation on all persons wishing to practice as psychologists to register with the Professional Board for Psychology currently administered by the South African Medical and Dental Council. The minimum requirement for registration as a psychologist is 5 years of academic training and a further year of practical training in a specialist field (clinical, counseling, industrial, or research psychology) at an approved institution under the direct supervision of a registered psychologist. The board also registers persons with a minimum of 3 academic years' training in psychology followed by 6 months' practical training in test administration as psychotechnicians.

Though the professional associations maintain a code of ethics based on that of the American Psychological Association, all persons registered with the professional board are subject to discipline in the event of their contravening the ethical restraints laid down by the board.

Research

Government Agencies. There are two semigovernmental agencies that provide extensive research facilities for psychologists, i.e., the Human Sciences Research Council and the Council for Scientific and Industrial Research (National Institute for Personnel Research). The Medical Research Council and the above-mentioned organizations offer various grants to different levels of research workers, especially in the fields of clinical psychology, psychosomatics, and neurophysiology.

Universities. Apart from university psychology departments, many universities have associated research institutes ranging from those concerned with primate research to some covering clinical services and others concentrating on neuropsychology. The Witwatersrand (Johannesburg), Stellenbosch, and Natal universities conduct research in physiological psychology and developmental, social, and clinical fields. The universities of Cape Town, Fort Hare, Pretoria, and Orange study personality, social developmental, and industrial psychology.

Private Research Centers. These are very few, although there are some large industrial concerns, such as the Chamber of Mines, that run excellent research centers employing various types of psychologists in research applied to industrial and organizational psychology.

Publications

Journals. There are three major journals in the field: The *South African Journal of Psychology* is published once a year by the SAPA, P. O. Box 4292, Johannesburg, South Africa.

Psychologia Africana is published at irregular intervals by the National Institute for Personnel Research, P. O. Box 10319, Johannesburg, South Africa.

The *Journal of Behavioral Science* is published at irregular intervals by the Psychological Society, University of Natal, Durban, South Africa.

Books. Few, if any, scholarly books for the profession are published locally. Educational textbooks are published (usually in Afrikaans) at the rate of about one every other year.

Occupational Distribution

There are over 1,000 psychologists in South Africa. They are employed by universities, research centers, educational systems, hospitals, and industry.

Opportunities for Foreign Psychologists

Foreign-trained psychologists may work in South Africa under the control of a registered psychologist until such time as they can obtain registration themselves. There is provision for conditional and also interim registration of some foreign-trained psychologists. In most cases, the psychologist would need to work in an approved institution for 2 years before taking a short formal examination set by the professional board. It is possible in some instances that where reciprocal arrangements exist, the board will directly recognize foreign training for purposes of registration.

Inquiries should be directed via consular services to the South African Medical and Dental Council, Professional Board of Psychology. Psychologists interested in temporary research and/or visiting professorships should write directly to a particular university in South Africa.

Spain[1]

Introduction

The first laboratory of experimental psychology was established in 1885 at Madrid University by José Simarra. In 1918 the Instituto de Orientación Profesional (Institute of Vocational Orientation), later called Instituto de Psicotécnica (Psychotechnical Institute), was established in Barcelona under the leadership of Emilio Mira. In 1920 the Instituto Nacional de Psicología Aplicada (National Institute of Applied Psychology) was organized in Madrid by José Germain.

In 1949, after the civil war (1936–1939), the National Research Council developed a department of psychology. At the present time, Spanish psychologists take an active part in scientific research and collaborate with their European and American colleagues.

National Organization

The Spanish organization for psychologists is the Sociedad Española de Psicología. Its address is:

Instituto de Psicología Aplicada
Ciudad Universitaria
Madrid 3, Spain

The official language is Spanish.

---

[1] Based on information supplied by José Mallart, secretary-general, Sociedad Española de Psicología, and other sources.

Internal Structure

The sociedad has four divisions: (1) experimental psychology, (2) clinical psychology, (3) industrial psychology, and (4) educational psychology.

The aims of the sociedad are (1) to promote scientific psychology and (2) to promote the exchange of information and ideas among Spanish and foreign psychologists.

The governing bodies of the sociedad are the general assembly and the executive council (la junta directiva).

Membership

The total membership is over 1,300. There are six categories of members: (1) charter members; (2) regular members, who possess the title of psychologist, based on a university degree; (3) titular members, who in addition to the title of psychologist have been active as university instructors, researchers, or applied psychologists for at least 3 years; (4) corresponding members; (5) honorary members; and (6) supporting members.

Major Activities

The main activities of the sociedad include the organization of symposia and conferences, and publications.

Education and Training

Twelve universities in Spain offer training in psychology at the graduate level; there are three in Madrid, three in Barcelona, two in Salamanca, and one each in Valencia, Santiago, La Laguna, and Pamplona. The degrees issued by these universities are as follows: The degrees of licenciado and doctor are granted by 1 university; the degree of diplomado (3 years in the university and additional professional training) is granted by 10 universities; the degree diplomado in applied psychology (clinical, industrial, educational) is granted by 2 institutes in the universities of Madrid and Barcelona. It is a postgraduate degree.

There are other private and governmental programs of training for the armed forces and industrial, educational, and clinical counseling without degrees.

At the present time, student enrollments are as follows: diplomado level—about 10,000 students; licenciado level—about 2,000 students; diplomado in applied psychology level—about 400 students; doctor level—about 100 students.

All Spanish universities are governmental except two (Salamanca and Pamplona). The degrees of these two private universities have to be validated for accreditation by means of an examination before a jury composed of professors of psychology from both the governmental and the private universities.

Legal Status

Teaching, research, and professional activities can be legally undertaken only by licenciados and doctors. Since these degrees are granted by universities owned and/or controlled by the Spanish government, these degrees are tantamount to a license.

There is an ethical code elaborated by the national psychological organization and published in *Revista de Psicología General y Aplicada*. There are other professional regulations concerning the use of tests, rights of the clients, etc., published in *Revista de Psicología General y Aplicada*.

Research

All universities offer grants and research fellowships. The research covers human and animal psychology, theoretical and applied psychology, and experimental and clinical psychology. The Instituto Nacional de Aplicada Psicología y Psicotécnia (the National Institute for Applied Psychology and Psychotechnics) conducts research in vocational guidance, industrial and clinical psychology, psychometrics, etc.

Some governmental agencies are involved in clinical and educational psychology, guidance counseling, and psychometrics.

Substantial financial support for research comes from the Higher Council for Scientific Research and several private foundations.

Publications

Journals. Three major journals are published in Spain:

The quarterly, *Revista de Psicología General y Aplicada* is published by the Instituto Nacional de Psicología, Ciudad Universitaria, Madrid, Spain.

The *Anuario de Psicología* is published by the Universidad de Barcelona, three issues per year.

Alta Dirección is published four times a year.

Books. Several Spanish publishing houses issue scholarly psychological books in the original language and in translation.

Occupational Distribution

Spanish psychologists work in a variety of fields. A large percentage teach in the universities and high schools. A great many work in the educational system as school psychologists and guidance counselors. Spanish clinical psychologists work in hospitals and clinics and engage in private practice. Many Spanish psychologists work in vocational guidance, personnel, and industrial psychology.

Opportunities for Foreign Psychologists

Foreign psychologists with university degrees equivalent to a master's or doctorate can work in private institutions and agencies in Spain. For professional and research activities in universities and governmental institutions, the validation of this degree by a Spanish university is required.

Inquiries should be directed to Spanish consulates.

Sweden[1]

National Organization

Practically all Swedish psychologists are members of their national organization, the

Swedish Psychological Association
Becks Judar Vägen 45–47
13100 Nacka
Sweden

The official language is Swedish.

Internal Structure

The governing body of the association is the executive committee, elected by the general assembly.

Membership

The total number of members is over 1,000. Holders of candidate degrees or licentiates or doctorates in psychology are admitted as members of the association.

The association has three divisions: (1) school and educational psychology, (2) industrial psychology, and (3) clinical psychology.

---

[1]Based on information supplied by various sources.

Major Activities

The main activities of the association are: (1) joint conferences with the other Scandinavian psychological associations (of Denmark, Finland, and Norway), and (2) joint publications with the other Scandinavian psychological associations.

Education and Training

Five Swedish universities offer undergraduate and graduate training in psychology. These universities are the University of Göteberg, the University of Lund, the University of Stockholm, the University of Mmeå, and the University of Uppsala.

As early as the 2nd year of undergraduate studies a distinction is made between theoretical and applied careers in psychology. Those who choose a theoretical career with the aim of becoming researchers or teachers are trained in a variety of psychological fields and in research. At the end of their 3rd year of studies, they receive the candidate diploma in theoretical psychology. Those who choose applied psychology are given the opportunity to specialize in clinical, industrial, or educational psychology. At the end of their 3rd year of studies, they receive the diploma of candidate in applied psychology. The candidate degrees entitle their holders to teach psychology in high schools and to work as assistant psychologists in appropriate research or service institutions.

Most candidates continue their advanced studies in either theoretical or applied areas. At present there are about 400 students in a 3- to 4-year program that leads to the high degree of licentiate. The training in applied fields is combined with a practicum.

The holders of the title of licentiate in psychology are recognized as fully qualified psychologists. They may, if they wish, submit a dissertation for the doctor's degree.

All programs in psychology are approved by the Swedish government.

Legal Status

Holders of the degree of candidate in psychology can be gainfully employed as assistant psychologists; holders of licentiate or doctorate degrees are recognized as psychologists. Both degrees are awarded by state-owned universities and are certified by the Swedish Psychological Association, which has clearly stated professional and ethical rules. This certification is generally recognized.

Research

The centers of research in Sweden are the Swedish Council for Social Science Research in Stockholm, the Swedish Medical Research Council in Uppsala, the Personnel Administration Council in Stockholm, and various mental health centers and industrial psychology institutes.

All Swedish universities are actively engaged in experimental studies in basic and applied fields. The University of Stockholm conducts extensive research in comparative and physiological psychology, the University of Lund mainly in clinical and personality psychology, etc.

Publications

The Swedish Psychological Association publishes (in cooperation with the Danish, Finnish, and Norwegian psychological associations) the *Scandinavian Journal of Psychology*, a quarterly, and the *Nordisk Psykologi*.

Occupational Distribution

Swedish psychologists teach in universities and high schools, conduct research, and work in a variety of fields or in applied psychology as clinicians.

Opportunities for Foreign Psychologists

Foreign psychologists wishing to work in Sweden on a temporary basis as visiting professors or researchers may contact the Swedish Psychological Association or one of the universities.

Switzerland[1]

Introduction

Switzerland, the little country with a total population of 6,000,000, has made a unique contribution to psychology. The two giants in psychology, Carl Gustav Jung and Jean Piaget, are Swiss, the first one German-Swiss and the other French-Swiss. Jung's main contribution was to personality theory and clinical psychology; Piaget's main work has been developmental and cognitive studies.

E. Claparede, E. Blender, H. Rorschach, L. Szondi, M. Boss, and scores of Swiss psychologists and psychiatrists have greatly influenced European and American psychology and have made a lasting contribution to experimental, cognitive, developmental, and educational psychology, as well as to projective methods, psychoanalysis, and existentialism.

National Organizations

The temporary address of the national psychological organization is:

Schweizerische Gesellschaft für Psychologie
Société Suisse de Psychologie
Les Courbes
CH-1181 Gilly
Switzerland

The official languages are German and French.

[1]Based on information supplied by Remy Droz, president, Swiss Society of Psychology, and other sources.

There is also another organization, the Schweizerischer Berufsverband für Angewandte Psychologie.

Internal Structure

All important decisions are taken by the general assembly of the Swiss Society of Psychology; an executive committee takes care of current problems. There is usually one yearly meeting of the general assembly and four to six meetings of the committee. The president and the members of the committee are elected by direct vote of the general assembly. Ad hoc commissions can be created by the committee or by the general assembly.

Membership

The membership totals 363 with the following divisions: ordinary members— 317, extraordinary members—41, honorary members—5 (plus one honorary president).

Membership Requirements

Honorary members are elected by the general assembly. Ordinary members must hold a university degree in psychology or a university degree with psychology as a main field of study; minimal duration of studies in psychology is 4 years. Alternatively, ordinary members may complete studies in medicine with a subsequent specialization in psychiatry (FMH). Extraordinary members may participate in any other training in psychology or in studies at university level in a field other than psychology.

Major Activities

The society's major activities consist of annual meetings, usually held in the spring, for a duration of 2 days. The time is used for an administrative meeting and for scientific communications or for a thematic symposium. Since about 80% of the members are working as clinical psychologists, themes are usually chosen from applied psychology.

Periodical meetings of psychologists and nonmembers of the society who are working in the field of psychological research are held; these involve scientific communications, discussions on research policy and research coordination, etc. Irregularly, workshops centered on a particular subject are also held.

The society also publishes the *Schweizerische Zeitschrift für Psychologie und ihre Anwendungen* (published by Verlag Hans Huber, Bern); one volume per year is issued, containing original research articles and book reviews.

Education and Training

There are seven universities in Switzerland in Basel, Bern, Fribourg, Geneva, Lausanne, Neuchâtel, and Zurich. Full psychological training is offered in Bern, Fribourg, and Zurich. Geneva, Lausanne, and Fribourg offer training in clinical, educational, and industrial psychology. Advanced training in industrial psychology is offered by the University of St. Gall, the Eidgenossische Hochschule, Zurich, and the Ecole Polytechnique Fédérale, Lausanne.

The usual titles (degrees) granted by Swiss universities are license in psychology, or Lic. Phil. (about 4 years of training), and doctorate in psychology, or Dr. Phil. (more than 4 years).

Special diplomas are either postgraduate (1 year after the license) or intermediary titles (e.g., 2 years or 4 years of training). Advanced training and specializations are offered as follows: Basel—none; Bern—research, clinical psychology, psychology of labor/industrial psychology, professional guidance; Fribourg—industrial psychology, professional guidance, school psychology; Geneva—research (experimental and genetic psychology), clinical psychology, educational psychology, psychopathology of language; Lausanne—professional guidance; Neuchâtel—psychology of labor/industrial psychol-

ogy (basic training either in Geneva or in Lausanne); Zurich—
research, clinical psychology, applied psychology, social
psychology, anthropological psychology; Zurich (Eidgenossische Technische Hochschule)—biological psychology.
The intensity of specialization is variable from one university to the other. The number of students in psychology as a
main field in 1978 in the universities is approximated as follows: Basel—85, Bern—276, Fribourg—182, Lausanne—122,
Geneva—489, Neuchâtel—3, Zurich—748.

Degrees obtained are approximated as follows: Basel—
4, Bern—15, Fribourg—10, Geneva—100, Lausanne—6,
Neuchâtel—6, Zurich—100.

Legal Status

In some cases, the Société Suisse de Psychologie delivers
"diplomas" that attest a sufficient training in psychology. This
title has no legal validity. A professional ethical code also exists;
a "court of honor" (composed of members of this society)
judges cases concerning members of the society. Maximum
penalty can be exclusion from the society.

Research

Most research is done in universities and in the two
polytechnical schools; a large part of this research is financed
by the Fonds National Suisse de la Recherche Scientifique, a
federally financed private foundation that is controlled by the
universities.

Main fields of research are cognitive psychology, social
and developmental psychology, industrial psychology, and
clinical psychology. The only institution of a private character
and of more than local importance is the C. G. Jung Institute
(Zurich), which also provides postgraduate training within a
specific field.

Publications

Swiss publishers, among them Karger and Huber, publish several scholarly books in psychology, both original works and translations.

Occupational Distribution

The majority of the 1,000 or more Swiss psychologists work in the clinical field in hospitals, clinics, and health centers in cooperation with psychiatrists and social workers. Some clinical psychologists are in private practice. Many Swiss psychologists work in industry as personnel, organizational, and job analysis experts. Very few teach in schools of higher learning.

Opportunities for Foreign Psychologists

Due to temporary limitations on foreign manpower, Switzerland does not hire foreign psychologists. However, visiting research and teaching positions for outstanding psychologists could be available. Inquiries should be addressed to a particular university.

Syria[1]

There is no psychological association in the Syrian Arab Republic. The two national universities in Aleppo and Damascus offer courses in psychology but do not train psychologists. The Damascus University offers courses in psychology in the framework of the department of education, liberal arts, and business administration.

There have been efforts to enlarge the scope of teaching psychology. Some Syrian students study psychology abroad, mostly in France.

Foreign psychologists interested in permanent or temporary job opportunities in Syria should contact a Syrian consulate.

[1]Based on information supplied by various sources.

Turkey[1]

National Organization

The national psychological organization is the Turkish Psychological Association (TPA)

        Turkish Psychological Association (TPA)
        c/o Professor N. Arkun
        Institute of Psychology
        Faculty of Letters, University of Istanbul
        Beyazit, Istanbul, Turkey

The official language is Turkish.

Internal Structure

The responsibilities of the executive committee are similar to that of the American Psychological Association (APA); the committee is elected by the membership, consisting of about 55 members.

Membership

There is no distinction in types of membership nor are there any sections or divisions of special-interest groups within the membership. Requirements for membership are that the candidate hold at least a B.A. degree in psychology.

---

[1]Based on information supplied by Nezahat Arkun, president of the Turkish Psychological Association, and other sources.

Major Activities

The association holds an annual meeting during the fall and also organizes group seminars and conferences.

Education and Training

All seven universities in Turkey offer training in psychology. They grant a degree similar to a B.A. in psychology and a higher degree similar to a Ph.D. in psychology. The Istanbul University offers courses in developmental, experimental, and social psychology. The Middle East Technical University (METU) emphasizes clinical, educational, and social psychology.

Legal Status

Attempts are being made by the TPA to place psychology on a legal foundation, but this is still in its initial stage.

Research and Publication

Research in psychology is being done only at the universities, which support and give grants for these activities; there are, however, no private research centers yet.

There is only one journal published by the Institute of Experimental Psychology in Istanbul University. Its name is *Istanbul Studies in Experimental Psychology,* University of Istanbul. It is an annual journal and almost all psychologists publish their work in this journal. Besides this there is a psychological bulletin, which is a newsletter published biannually by TPA.

Occupational Distribution

Most Turkish psychologists teach at the universities, although some work in the educational system as guidance counselors and school psychologists and, in addition, as clinical psychologists in hospitals. A few are also in private practice.

Opportunities for Foreign Psychologists

Turkey welcomes foreign experts in clinical and counseling psychology as well as university professors—all on a visiting basis. For information, one must write to a Turkish university or consult a Turkish consular service.

Ukrainian Soviet Socialist Republic[1]

National Organization

Ukrainian psychologists are members of the
    Soviet Psychological Association
    Institute of General and Educational Psychology
    University of Moscow
    20 Karl Marx Avenue
    Moscow K-9, USSR
The official languages are Ukrainian and Russian.

Research

The Psychology Research Institute, Ministry of Education of the Ukrainian SSR, at 2 Khalturin Street, Kiev, Ukrainian SSR, 252033, is the main center of psychological research in the Ukraine.

The institute consists of laboratories, workshops, and a science library, holding more than 60,000 books and 3,000 microfilms on psychology.

The self-governing organ of the institute is the academic council, which includes the leading scientists of the institute.

---

[1]Based on information supplied by Valdimir N. Martynenko, ambassador extraordinary and plenipotentiary, Permanent Mission of the Ukrainian Soviet Socialist Republic to the United Nations, and other sources. Additional information is given in the section on the USSR.

The total number of scientists employed by the institute is 132.

The institute has several laboratories, among them laboratories for methodology of psychological studies, personality psychology, preschool education psychology, psychology of learning, educational psychology, psychology of labor—learning and education, psychology of professional guidance, social psychology, psychology of communication, psychology of disturbed children, psychology of the hard of hearing, psychophysiology, and psychology of training people to work with computers.

Major Activities

The institute organizes annual scientific conferences, scientific meetings on various specific subjects of psychology, monthly seminars in laboratories, scientific discussion on some topical problems of psychology, and current psychological literature.

The institute is a state institution and it is financed from the state budget. The institute also concludes contracts to conduct research studies with various industrial and educational organizations throughout the country.

Publications

Psychology, in the Ukrainian language, is published annually at 2 Khalturin Street, Kiev, Ukrainian SSR, 252033.

In each year 5−7 books, 16−20 pamphlets, and 250 articles on various aspects of psychology are published.

Union of Soviet Socialist Republics (USSR)[1]

Introduction

The origins of psychology in Russia go back 200 years to Lomonosov's three-components theory of color vision in 1757. The other forerunners of Russian psychology, among them Dobrolyubov, Herzen (Gertsen), and Radishtcher, represent a variety of idealistic, mentalistic, and prescientific theories.

Sechenov's *Reflexes of the Cerebrum,* published in 1863, signals the birth of Russian scientific psychology. Sechenov has set the path for the neurophysiological orientation of Pavlov, Bekhterev, and the future generations of Russian psychologists.

The first psychophysiological laboratory in Russia was established in 1886 by Bekhterev, in Kazan. In 1893 Bekhterev was appointed to the neuropathology and psychiatry division of the Academy of Military Science in Petersburg. His *Objective Psychology,* published in 1907, advocated a materialistic and mechanistic approach to psychology.

In 1896 Pavlov was appointed head of the physiology department of the Medico-Surgical Academy, and in 1904 he won the Nobel Prize. Pavlov's experimental studies and his theory of conditioned reflexes have been a milestone in the

[1]Based on information supplied by Prof. B. F. Lomov, Psychological Institute of the USSR Academy of Sciences, and other sources.

history of science and greatly influenced psychological research in Russia and the world over.

The Bolshevik revolution in 1917 affected all areas of Russian science, including psychology. It introduced the distinct approach of dialectical materialism developed by Marx, Engels, and Lenin as a binding philosophy.

According to Marx, "it is not consciousness that determines life but life that determines consciousness." Marx rejected the mechanistic-materialistic doctrine that "men are the product of circumstances." Marx stressed the bipolar nature of the environment versus psyche processes. Not only are men changed by circumstances, they change the circumstances. According to Lenin, sensation "is connected with a particular kind of process in matter" and dialectical materialism gives impetus to continuous experimentation. Lenin quoted Engels as being "opposed to the 'vulgar' materialism." While the existence of mind is dependent upon that of the body, it is not a mechanical but a dialectical interaction. Small wonder that Lenin favored Pavlov's theories and, after years of search, all Soviet psychologists have endeavored to combine the Marx-Lenin theories with Pavlov's theories on conditioning.

One may distinguish four phases in the development of Soviet psychology. The first period started with the Bolshevik revolution in 1917 and with the struggle against mentalism and idealism. Bekhterev, Blonskii, Kornilov, and others have interpreted the Marx-Engels-Lenin theory and viewed all activities as a reflection of the objective world. Kornilov's theory of "reactology" presented psyche as a mere "subjective reflection" of nervous processes.

In their efforts to reinterpret psychology on more precise Marxist lines, Ukhtomski, Vygotski, Leontyev, Luria, and others stressed the sociocultural aspects and historical perspectives in psychology. Vygotski maintained that personality development (the intrapsychological processes) is a product of historical development (interpsychological processes). According to Leontyev, behavior is a function of sociocultural factors viewed in historical sequence.

In the third period, Soviet psychologists, among them Rubinstein, Smirnov, Lomov, and Teplov, endeavored to combine experimental studies in diverse areas of psychology—such as developmental and educational psychology, sensation and perception, drives and conditioning—with the Marxist-Leninist dialectical materialism. An outstanding work in this field is S. R. Rubinstein's *Being and Consciousness*.

In 1950 the Joint Conference of the Soviet Academy of Medical Sciences and the Academy of Science in the USSR decreed a return to Pavlov and demanded that psychological studies be based on Pavlov's theories of higher nervous activity and conditioned reflexes. The conference decided to "reconstruct on the basis of Pavlov's teachings: physiology, psychology, pathology, psychiatry, etc." Bykov, Luria, Leontyev, Ivanov, Smolenski, Yaroshevski, Anokhin, Ananyev, Asratyan, and scores of others embarked upon the road to a basically Pavlovian psychology with a due consideration of the tenets of the Marxist-Leninist philosophy. In 1959 the Soviet Academy of Pedagogical Science published the following path-setting collective work in psychology: Ananyev, B. G., Kostyuk, G. S., Leontyev, A. N., Luria, A. R., Menchinskaya, N. A., Rubinshtein, S. L., Smirnov, A. A., Teplov, B. M., and Shemyakin, F. N. (Eds.), *The Science of Psychology* (Russian). Moscow: Academy of Pedagogical Science, 1959.

National Organization

The Soviet Psychological Association was formed in 1957. Its address is:

Soviet Psychological Association
Institute of General and Educational Psychology
University of Moscow
20 Karl Marx Avenue
Moscow K-9, USSR

The official language is Russian.

Internal Structure

Each of the republics that belongs to the Union of Soviet Socialist Republics has its own national organization, e.g., Ukrainian, Byelorussian, Gengian, Armenian, etc. The business of each organization is conducted in the national language.

The ruling body of the Soviet association is its executive committee.

Membership

There are about 2,000 psychologists in the Soviet Union; all of them are members of the association. Every practicing psychologist who teaches psychology or works in a laboratory or a clinic is eligible for membership in the association.

Divisions

The Soviet Psychological Association has nine divisions, as follows: (1) general psychology, which includes conditioning, perception, personality, and research methods; (2) developmental psychology; (3) educational psychology; (4) comparative psychology; (5) defectology, or special psychology, which deals with intellectual, sensory, motor, and other children's handicaps; (6) medical (clinical) psychology; (7) industrial psychology; (8) physical education and sports psychology; and (9) history of psychology.

Major Activities

The association requires all-union conferences. The first all-union conference was held in Moscow, June 20–July 4, 1959. The association cooperates with all universities and research centers in the USSR. It publishes journals and actively participates in international conferences and exchanges of scientific information.

Education and Training

All Soviet universities and several institutions of higher learning, such as the pedagogical institutes and medical schools, technical and engineering training centers, etc., offer a variety of courses in every field of psychology. Starting with the 2nd year of university programs, the emphasis is on independent research, and experimental studies form the backbone of both undergraduate and graduate work. The graduating students receive a diploma in psychology.

Graduate psychology students, called aspirants, receive advanced training in a specialized field of their choice. Toward the end of a 3-year program, they must pass appropriate examinations and submit a dissertation. Upon the acceptance of the thesis, the aspirant is awarded the title of candidate of science. They may pursue their studies toward the doctor of science degree, which is granted on the basis of a dissertation that represents a significant contribution to psychological science. The main training centers are the Moscow and Leningrad universities.

Legal Status

Since all schools, all research centers, and all educational, industrial, and other organizations belong to the state, a diploma in psychology entitles one to call himself a psychologist and hold a junior position in a university, research center, or other institution. The candidate of science and doctor of science degrees entitle their holders to a higher level of employment. The doctoral degree also entitles the holder to a supervisory position in the field of psychology.

Research

All research in the Soviet Union is sponsored either by the government of the Soviet Union or by the governments of the republics that are parts of the union. The main centers of research are:

1. The Academy of Pedagogical Sciences of the USSR and its (a) Moscow Institute of Psychology and (b) Psychology Department of the Institute of Philosophy.
2. The Academy of Science of the USSR and its institutes: (a) the Pavlov Institute of Physiology, Leningrad, (b) the Institute of Neurophysiology and Higher Nervous Activity, (c) the Sechenov Institute of Evolutionary Psychology.
3. The Academy of Medical Sciences of the USSR and its various institutes, especially (a) the Institute of Psychiatry and (b) the Brain Institute.
4. The Institute of Psychology of the Ministry of Education of the Ukrainian SSR, Kiev.
5. The Academy of Science of the Russian SSR and its (a) Moscow Institute of Defectology and (b) Leningrad Institute of Education.
6. The Uznadze Institute of Psychology of the Academy of Science of Georgian SSR, Tiflis.

In addition, there are scores of research centers all around the country, most of them affiliated with universities. Highly diversified research is conducted by the universities of Moscow, Leningrad, Tiflis, Kiev, and many others.

The main body of current Soviet research is directed toward further development of Pavlov's conditioning combined with the dialectical philosophy of Marx and Lenin. Psychophysiology is apparently the best developed branch, including such areas as sensation, perception, electroencephalography, memory, psycholinguistics, speech, thinking, cybernetics, mathematical psychology, information theory, developmental and educational psychology, psychopathology, and ergonomics.

One of the outstanding features of Soviet research is the special attention given to *interoceptive conditioning,* in which the conditioned stimulus is internal and applied to inner organs, in contradistinction to the usual exteroceptive stimuli applied to the external endings of sensory apparatus.

Psycholinguistics and the study of the verbal (second) signaling system as a typically human type of conditioning has been another favorite research area in the Soviet Union.

Soviet psychologists have also conducted extensive research concerning the *orienting* reflex. These studies include electroencephalographic, electromyographic, electrodermal, vascular, sensory, and other areas of research.

Applied experimental psychology plays a significant role in the Soviet Union. Research in psychology delves into psychosomatic processes, hypertension, experimental neuroses, psychopharmacology, central focal brain lesions, and many other issues.

Psychotherapeutic research is mainly represented by studies on verbal suggestion, experimental hypnosis, and reeducation of mental patients by conditioning.

Human engineering and application of the study of man's psychophysiological abilities to the design of machinery play an important role in the state-owned industry of the USSR.

Publications

Journals. Soviet psychological studies are published in several journals; among them: *Voprosy Psikhologii* (Problems of Psychology), *Voprosy Filosofii* (Problems of Philosophy), *Zhurnal Vyshey Nervnoy Dieyatelnosti* (Journal of Higher Nervous Activity), and many other journals, annual reports, and proceedings of seminars and scientific conferences.

Books. The above-mentioned scientific academies have their own publication houses. The number of books published in psychology and related areas in the Soviet Union is second only to that in the United States.

Occupational Distribution

All Soviet psychologists are governmental employees. Most of them are associated with research organizations, universities and other schools of higher learning, especially pedagogical institutes. Many of them work in the school system, industry, and administration, especially human engineering, organization, and management.

Clinical psychologists are mostly involved in research in medical centers, hospitals, etc. Most of the research follows Pavlov neurophysiological theories, and a great deal of work is devoted to biochemical factors of mental disorders.

Opportunities for Foreign Psychologists

Foreign psychologists who wish to visit the Soviet Union and get acquainted with the Soviet psychology or conduct research or give lectures in one of the USSR universities must contact a Soviet consulate.

United Kingdom[1]

Introduction

Hardly any other nation has done more for the development of psychology as an empirical science. British philosophers, especially J. Locke and D. Hume, have introduced empiricism, followed by the associationism of David Hartley, Thomas T. Reid, J. Stewart, and Thomas Brown, and in the 19th century by James Mill, J. S. Mill, and Alexander Bain. John Stuart Mill's ideas were further developed by W. Wundt in Germany, Bain's ideas have influenced W. James and E. L. Thorndike in the United States, and I.P. Pavlov's and V. Bekhterev's conditioning is undoubtedly indebted to British associationists.

The evolutionary approach to human nature and the use of animal subjects for drawing of comparative influences originates with the theories of two British scientists, Charles Darwin and Thomas H. Huxley. S. Freud and I. M. Sechenov, W. Stern and P. Janet, C. L. Hull and J. Piaget, and hardly any psychologist in the latter part of the 19th and in the 20th century could escape the pervasive influence of the theory of evolution. The origins of comparative psychology are linked with the pioneering work of Spalding and Lloyd Morgan.

British scientists have made a lasting contribution to neurophysiology and have broken the ground for a scientific interpretation of motor and sensory processes. Charles Bull, Hughlings Jackson, Charles Sherrington, to mention only a few, are the fathers of modern physiological psychology.

[1]Based on information supplied by Ralph R. Hetherington, secretary-general of the British Psychological Society, and other sources.

Although the best-known intelligence tests are associated with the name of the French psychologist Alfred Binet, the idea of mental measurements and the application of statistical methods in assessing individual differences must be credited to Francis Galton and Karl Pearson. Charles Spearman published the first group intelligence test in 1907, and he and Cyril Bartt developed theories of human intelligence. The statistical analysis of variance, one of the indispensable tools in contemporary psychological research, was developed by R. A. Fisher.

National Organization

The national psychological organization of the United Kingdom of Great Britain and Northern Ireland is the
British Psychological Society
18–19 Albemarle Street
London WIX 4DN
England
The official language is English.

Internal Structure

The decision-making body within the society is the general meeting, which all members of the society have a right to attend. A special general meeting may be called at any time by the honorary general secretary, at the request of the president, the council, or any 50 members. An annual general meeting must be held once in every calendar year at which the society's accounts and reports of the council and auditors must be considered and officers and members of the council elected.

The council is the executive committee of the society and is responsible for all decisions concerning the society's operations. Its constitution has been carefully designed to ensure representation of branches, sections, and divisions of the society, in addition to the 12 members elected by members of the society at the annual general meeting. The council meets about four times a year and is required to make an annual report to members of the society. The council appoints all boards and standing committees and lays down their terms of reference.

The finance and general purposes standing committee has the functions of forward planning, continuous budgetary control, and allocation of funds, subject to the approval of the council, and it negotiates contracts of employment with all staff in the secretariat.

Some of the council's executive responsibilities have been delegated to other groups within the society. These are the scientific affairs board and the professional affairs board.

The constitution of the boards ensures that sections and editors of journals have places on the scientific affairs board, and that divisions are represented on the professional affairs board. Both boards have some members appointed by the council and others appointed by members of the society.

The scientific affairs board, on behalf of the council, must (1) plan, arrange, and organize the scientific meetings and conferences of the society; (2) stimulate new interests and ventures, including those of small groups of psychologists; (3) stimulate the exchange of psychological knowledge between psychologists of different countries; (4) keep scientific policies concerning publication of psychological journals by the society under continuing review; (5) promote and, where appropriate, sponsor occasional publications, especially of scientific papers, reviews, and reports; (6) be concerned with scientific policies and activities of interest to two or more sections, and advise on scientific matters at the request of a section or sections; (7) attract such income to the funds of the society as may be conducive to carrying out, maintaining, and extending the activities of the society sponsored by the board; (8) make appropriate financial arrangements; (9) make arrangements for the annual award of the Spearman Medal; and (10) make arrangements for the annual Myers Lecture.

The board has also to advise the council on scientific research, the library, publications, the institution of awards and prizes, and the need for new sections of the society.

The professional affairs board, on behalf of the Council,

must (1) inquire, as may be appropriate, into matters concerning the practice of psychology by psychologists; (2) be able to submit evidence to public or private bodies on matters concerning the practice of psychology; (3) be concerned with policies and activities of interest to two or more divisions of the society; (4) interpret the society's policies approved by the council with regard to courses of postgraduate professional training in psychology (a) by inquiring into and considering proposals for new courses or for the reorganization of courses of training in the practice of psychology and (b) by approving such proposals as may be appropriate; (5) be able to institute and organize courses of training (a) in the practice of psychology by psychologists and (b) in the use of psychological techniques by others; (6) consider and, if thought fit, approve the recommendations of the standing committee on test standards of the council regarding approval by the society of courses of training in the use of psychological tests; (7) be able to plan, organize, and arrange meetings and conferences concerned with the practice of psychology; (8) be concerned with establishing and maintaining relations with the national societies of psychology in other countries for the exchange of knowledge and information about psychological practice; (9) promote and, where appropriate, sponsor occasional publications on matters of interest for the practice of psychology; (10) be concerned with attracting such income as may be conducive to carrying out, maintaining, and extending the activities of the society sponsored by the board; and (11) make appropriate financial arrangements.

The board has also to advise the council on research in applied psychology, professional practice, postgraduate training, professional examinations, the use of tests, the need for new divisions within the society, and the scale of fees that might be charged by the society for its services.

In terms of its charter, the society is entitled to conduct examinations and to issue certificates and diplomas to persons qualified to practice and teach psychology. The society's board of examiners is appointed by the council to undertake this task.

The board is currently responsible for running the society's diploma in clinical psychology and will shortly be undertaking the society's new diploma in developmental and educational psychology. The board has now been asked to arrange and conduct examinations for candidates for graduate membership of the society in whose cases additional assessments of their qualifications in psychology prove necessary.

Membership

The total number of members is 6,491, divided into the following categories: honorary fellows—21, fellows—383, associates—1,871, graduate members—2,481, ordinary members—302, foreign affiliates—84, subscribers—112, and student subscribers—1,237.

The British Psychological Society has six special-interest sections, as follows: medical—375, educational—776, occupational—529, social—517, mathematical and statistical—290, and developmental—550. It also has four divisions that represent professional groups, as follows: educational and child (England)—450, educational and child (Scotland)—87, clinical—601, and occupational—146.

Membership Requirements

Candidates for membership must hold an honors degree in psychology at a British university or its equivalent.

Membership Requirements for Divisions. Recognized postgraduate training in the particular field concerned is required of candidates for membership in one of the divisions.

Major Activities

The society organizes an annual conference at Easter, sectional and divisional conferences, and refresher courses for professionals.

Education and Training

There are over 50 universities and other schools of higher learning in Great Britain and Northern Ireland, and practically all of them offer courses in several aspects of psychology. Most universities grant B.A. or B.S. degrees in psychology to students whose major concentration is psychology. An honors B.A. or B.Sc. in psychology entitles the holder for admission to membership in the British Psychological Society and recognition as a psychologist.

The curricula leading to the bachelor's degree in psychology vary considerably from one school to another; e.g., in some universities the curriculum emphasizes biological and neurophysiological foundations; others emphasize applied clinical or applied industrial courses; at still other schools sociological and cultural issues prevail, and psychology programs are associated with social sciences. British psychologists seem to avoid partisan and narrow ideological commitments, and their universities offer highly diversified programs.

Advanced physiological training leads to M.A., Ph.D., and senior doctorate degrees, and in some universities, to specialized professional diplomas. The advanced programs are offered by several major universities in specialized fields such as educational, clinical, occupational (industrial), and forensic, usually combined with a thorough study in psychological theory, research methodology, and other areas of nonapplied psychology.

The University of London and its colleges (Bedford, Birkbeck, and University College) and their Faculty of Arts and Faculty of Science offer degrees of master of philosophy in psychology and doctor of philosophy in several areas of academic psychology. Such departments and institutes of the university offer specialized and advanced training, e.g., the Department of Occupational Psychology and the Institute of Education. The Department of Social Psychology, affiliated with the School of Economics and Political Science, offers a highly diversified program in social development, social organization, communication, etc. Clinical psychologists receive their training at the psychology department associated with the Institute of Psychiatry, etc.

Practically all universities in the United Kingdom offer advanced programs and higher degrees in various fields of psychology. Several nonuniversity centers have advanced programs in psychology, among them the Tavistock Clinic and Institute of Human Relations in London. The Tavistock Clinic and Institute trains clinical and educational psychologists. The London Institute of Psychoanalysis offers a postgraduate training program. Anna Freud's Hempstead Clinic and the Loewenfeld Institute train child psychoanalysts, the first in classic psychoanalytic technique, the second in Melanie Klein's principles.

Legal Status

The British Psychological Society distinguishes between associate and graduate members. An associate member is a holder of a B.A. or B.Sc. degree with honors; a graduate member is a holder of Ph.D. degree or its equivalent. This distinction is usually accepted by public and private institutions that employ psychologists.

Research

All universities in the United Kingdom actively pursue basic and/or applied research. No area in psychology is omitted, and British psychologists substantially contribute to psychological theory and such issues as mathematical psychology and statistics, conditioning and learning, neurophysiology, sensation and perception, social developmental, personality, testing and measurement, and any other scientific issue in psychology. In addition, applied psychology, notably clinical, educational, and industrial, is well represented on the campuses.

Governmental agencies, among them the National Health

Service in England and Wales, the education departments for Scotland and Northern Ireland, and other public and private organizations offer support to basic and applied research.

Publications

British psychologists publish a great many scientific periodicals, and publication of scientific books in psychology is second only to that in the United States.

Occupational Distribution

The 10,000 or more British psychologists engage in every possible field of research, teaching, and practice of psychology. Psychologists employed by universities and other schools of higher education usually combine teaching with research.

Experimental psychologists have their own society—the Experimental Psychology Society. Also, the educational psychologists have their Association of Educational Psychologists. Clinical psychologists are represented by the National Health Service, and clinical child psychologists belong to the Association for Child Psychology and Psychiatry. Many clinical psychologists are associated with hospitals and other mental health services and research centers, and many are in private practice.

Governmental agencies and business enterprises employ a great many psychologists, especially in research.

Opportunities for Foreign Psychologists

Foreign psychologists interested in a visiting appointment in the United Kingdom universities should contact the Committee of Vice-Chancellors and Principals, the British Council, and/or the British consulates. To obtain permanent occupation in a university or an applied psychology agency, one must be able to obtain a permit for employment. For information, one must contact a British consulate.

United States of America[1]

Introduction

There are more psychologists in the United States than in any other five countries combined, and the well over 50,000 American psychologists are setting the stage in research and practice of psychology for the entire world. Numerically, they account for about one-third of the number of psychologists in the world and their intellectual production exceeds 50% of all written work in psychology. A British psychologist who was a disciple of a German psychologist and who in 1892 became an American professor is often called the father of American psychology. The man is Edward Bradford Titchener, Wilhelm Wundt's disciple, the founder of experimental psychology and exponent of structuralism at Cornell University.

Actually, psychology in the United States started somewhat earlier. William James, John Dewey, George Trumbull Ladd, and G. Stanley Hall were the first American psychologists. W. James's main work, *Principles of Psychology*, published in 1878, marks the birth of a typically American psychology. James's philosophical pragmatism and psychological functionalism introduced the evolutionary-adjustment orientation. James viewed consciousness as a product

---

[1]Based on information supplied by C. Alan Boneau, acting executive officer, and Harley O. Preston, director, Office of External Affairs of the American Psychological Association, and other sources.

of evolution and perceived mental functions as a process of adjustment to the condition of life. This pragmatic functionalist view set the stage for generations of American psychologists. James's functionalism was diametrically opposed to the Wundt—Titchener introspectimistic-structural approach and broke ground for behaviorism and conditioning. Power and stress on change in behavior through conditioning was enthusiastically accepted by John Broadus Watson and scores of American psychologists who, under the banner of behaviorism, introduced objective research methods. As Watson put it in 1913, all "organisms, man and animal alike, do adjust themselves to their environments by means of heredity and habit equipment . . . in a system of psychology completely worked out given the stimulus and the response."

The stimulus-response (S-R) formula has since been widely used, although various meanings have been ascribed to it in the last six or seven decades by E. L. Thorndike, D. L. Hall, E. R. Guthrie, B. F. Skinner, E. C. Tolman, and scores of their faithful followers and dissident disciples. However, the spirit of pragmatism and functionalism, a rainbow variety of behavioristic and neobehavioristic approaches, and an emphasis on change and learning have remained the guidelines of most American psychologists devoted to experimental research and quantitative validation of observable behavior. American psychologists have unquestionably assumed the lead in basic research and applied fields of psychology.

The present-day American psychology cannot be conveniently divided into distinct "schools," for there has been a great deal of overlapping, mutual influences, and cross-fertilization of ideas. The main street remains pragmatic, decisively empirical, with a strong emphasis on experimental and statistical method. Conditioning and learning are still in the focus, but the study of cognitive processes has attracted a good deal of interest. The study on motivation and emotions, developmental and social psychology, and clinical and industrial psychology has been considerably influenced by learning theories. Physiological psychology and neurophysiology have become one of the major areas in psychological research, although to a somewhat lesser extent than in the Soviet Union (but second to nowhere else). Applied psychology, especially in the clinical field, has also come under the influence of quantitative research and conditioning, and the various methods of behavior modification bear witness to this development.

However, American psychology is far from being monolithic. In addition to the highly diversified and sophisticated network of behavioristic approaches, a great number of American psychologists favor a totally different approach to psychology. In 1908 G. Stanley Hall, then president of Clark University, invited S. Freud and his close associates to give a series of lectures at Clark University. Initially, psychoanalysis and its offshoots influenced only psychiatrists but gradually reached the influential Yale group (N. E. Miller, Dollard, Sears, Mowrer, and others) and spread from the learning theorists to clinical, developmental, and social psychologists. Currently, the various bounds of psychoanalysis inspire diversified research in child psychology, emotion, and motivation, and clinical theory and practice are greatly influenced by the teachings of Freud, Sullivan, Jung, Horney, Adler, Fromm, and others. Many American-born and some European immigrants have contributed to this psychoanalytically-oriented development.

American psychology was significantly enriched by the exodus of European psychologists who managed to escape the Nazi persecution. The leaders of the originally German Gestalt psychology, Köhler, Koffka, and Wertheimer, have brought a new approach to the study of perception, learning, and intelligence. Tolman tried to build bridges between learning and Gestalt, and Kurt Lewin developed his field and topological theories in his new homeland.

More recently, several American psychologists, notably C. Rogers and A. Maslov, have introduced a new trend into psychology of motivation called humanistic psychology. Although based on a new approach to research and practice, this new trend seems to be inspired by James's functionalism and Gordon Alpert's and Wilhelm Stern's ideas.

No idea and no area of research and practice are alien to American psychology. Psychology has become a powerful factor in the academic world with at least 100,000 students enrolled annually in undergraduate studies and almost 40,000 in graduate studies. Close to 2,500 Ph.D. degrees in psychology are granted annually and the fields of education, industry and technology, social relations, and mental health are considerably influenced by the indefatigable work of well-trained psychologists.

National Organization

The national psychological organization is the
American Psychological Association
1200 Seventh Street, N.W.
Washington, D. C. 20036
The official language is English.

Internal Structure

The chief governing body of the APA is the council of representatives, which includes representatives from each of the divisions and from affiliated state psychological associations. A board of directors, composed of the six officers of the APA (president, president-elect, past president, recording secretary, executive officer, and treasurer) and six council members elected by the council, is the administrative agent of the council and exercises general supervision over the affairs of the association.

Council of Representatives. The council of representatives is the legislative body of the association. The council has approximately 115 members inclusive of the board of directors and officers of the association.

The annual meeting of the council of representatives is held at the time and place of the national convention of the APA around the Labor Day weekend. An additional meeting is held in Washington, D.C., in January.

The members of the council represent the divisions of the American Psychological Association and the affiliated state psychological associations. Each fellow and member is eligible to vote, as is an associate in good standing for at least 5 consecutive years. The members of the council serve for 3 years.

Board of Directors. The board of directors supervises the work of the executive officer of the association and is responsible for the conduct of affairs of the association. The members of the board of directors review the agenda of the council of representatives and make recommendations to the council on these items.

Standing Boards and Committees. The standing boards and committees are the membership committee, the finance committee, the board of convention affairs, the committee on scientific and professional ethics and conduct, the election committee, the policy and planning board, the publications and communications board, the education and training board, the board of professional affairs, the board of scientific affairs, and the board of social and ethical responsibility for psychology.

The committee on scientific and professional ethics and conduct investigates complaints of unethical conduct. The committee formulates rules or principles of ethics for adoption by the association. The work of this committee, including information and recommendations on all cases before it, is kept confidential, but the committee cooperates with other committees and divisions of the association, the American Board of Professional Psychology, the ethics committee of the affiliated national and state associations, and licensing and certification boards in order to maintain ethical standards in the practice of psychology.

The education and training board supervises and coordinates the work of continuing committees involved in education and training of psychologists.

The board of professional affairs deals with psychology as a profession, and it is responsible for the standards of professional practice, relations with other professional groups, and application of psychology to the promotion of the public welfare.

The board of scientific affairs encourages and promotes scientific work in psychology and fosters relations with other scientific organizations.

The board of social and ethical responsibility for psychology is concerned with the role psychologists play in society at large, research in social issues, and the planning of public policy of the association.

The office of educational affairs appraises higher education and serves all American colleges and universities in a consulting capacity. The office cooperates with national and international organizations on matters of education and training and arranges visits of qualified psychologists to educational institutions. The office also publishes the names of graduate psychology departments. A special section of the office evaluates the programs, curricula, and professional training in universities and other centers. It conducts appraisal visits to these centers and prepares detailed reports to them and to the committee on accreditation. It develops guidelines and procedures for accreditation activities and adequacy of training and publishes the names of accredited programs in doctorate training and internships.

The office of professional affairs deals with psychology as a profession. It suggests guidelines for state legislation, specialty practice, and legal recognition of psychology as a mental health profession.

The office of scientific affairs deals with scientific aspects of psychology. It cooperates with other scientific organizations, federal government and private foundations, and committees. It encourages psychological research and the exchange of information among the various branches of science. This office develops and disseminates standards for such areas as instructional programs, psychological testing, and ethics of animal and human experimentalization, and coordinates and administers special projects in the area of scientific affairs. The staff of this office provides liaison with the board of scientific affairs and its committees and task forces.

All officers and members of the council and the board of directors are elected according to the Hare (preferential ballot) voting system.

Membership

The total number of APA members in 1978 was over 45,000. Membership categories are associate, member, and fellow. The various divisions are shown in Table 1, p. 259.

Membership Requirements

An associate must have completed 2 years of graduate work in psychology at a recognized graduate school and be engaged in work or graduate study that is primarily psychological in character; or must have received a master's degree in psychology from a recognized graduate school, have completed in addition 1 full year of professional work in psychology, and be engaged in work or graduate study that is primarily psychological in character.

A member must have received the doctoral degree based in part upon a psychological dissertation or from a program primarily psychological in content, and conferred by a graduate school of recognized standing.

Fellows must previously have been members for at least 1 full year, must have a doctoral degree in psychology and at least 5 years of acceptable experience beyond that degree in psychology, must hold membership in the nominating division, and must present evidence of unusual and outstanding contribution or performance in the field of psychology.

Any APA member may apply for membership in any division.

Major Activities

One of the main activities of the American Psychological Association is the promotion of psychology as a science. The association aims to serve human welfare by promotion of research and improvement of research methods. The APA is trying to improve the qualifications and usefulness of psychologists through high standards of professional ethics, conduct, education, and achievement. By increase and diffusion of psychological knowledge through meetings, professional contacts, and publications, the APA intends to advance scientific interests and inquiry in the application of research findings and thus to contribute to the promotion of the public welfare.

Education and Training

All 2,600 2- and 4-year courses in institutions of higher education offer at least one course in psychology. All but 14 of the 1,644 4-year institutions reporting to the U.S. Office of Education in 1970–71 (latest available figures) offered full baccalaureate programs. The figures from USOE's report on earned degrees conferred in 1970–1971 show the following: bachelor's—1,630, master's—301, doctorate—144.

The APA publication, *Graduate Study in Psychology 1975–1976*, includes over 400 institutions offering graduate-level training. The breakdown is as follows: master's —242, Ph.D.—173, Ed.D.—19, Psy.D.—1, D.A.—3.

A complete list of doctoral programs in clinical, counseling, and school psychology in 1978, approved by the American Psychological Association, is given in Table 2, pp. 260–262.

There are approximately 60 students per graduate (master's and doctoral) program, with a range of 4 to over 450. In 1978, about 8,000 students were enrolled in graduate M.A. and Ph.D. programs. Over 2,000 doctorates are annually granted, over half of them in clinical psychology.

Accreditation

The American Psychological Association is the internationally recognized agency that accredits doctoral training programs in the professional practice areas of clinical, counseling, and school psychology, and predoctoral internships in clinical and counseling psychology. During 1975, 101 doctoral training programs in clinical psychology, 21 doctoral training programs in counseling psychology, and 6 doctoral training programs in school psychology were accredited in the areas of clinical and counseling psychology. The APA accredits under the aegis of the Council on Post-secondary Accreditation (COPA), which controls university accreditation by recognizing certain accrediting agencies as having responsibility for specific educational fields. The association is also recognized by the U.S. Office of Education as the accrediting agency for doctoral training programs and predoctoral internships in clinical and counseling psychology.

Legal Status

The legal status of psychologists is determined by laws issued in every one of the 50 states. (See Table 3, pp. 263–266, and Table 4, p. 267 for characteristics of laws and provisions in the United States and in the Canadian provinces.)

Research

Every American school of higher education encourages research in a variety of fields. Two agencies of the federal government are particularly concerned with fostering research, namely, the National Institute of Mental Health, 5600 Fishers Lane, Rockville, Maryland 20852, and the National Science Foundation, Washington, D.C. 20550.

In addition, several public and private organizations and foundations offer considerable support to research in practically all areas of psychology.

Publications

Journals. The American Psychological Association publishes the following journals: *American Psychologist, Contemporary Psychology; Developmental Psychology; Journal of Abnormal Psychology; Journal of Applied Psychology; Journal of Comparative and Physiological Psychology; Journal of Consulting and Clinical Psychology; Journal of Counseling Psychology; Journal of Educational Psychology; Journal of Experimental Psychology: General; Journal of Experimental Psychology: Human Learning and Memory; Journal of Experimental Psychology: Human Perception and Performance; Journal of Experimental Psychology: Animal Behavior Processes; Journal of Personality and Social Psychology; Professional Psychology; Psychological Bulletin;* and *Psychological Review.* The APA also publishes *Psychological Abstracts,* the *APA Monitor,* a monthly employment bulletin, the *APA Biographical Directory,* the *Convention Program,* and the *JSAS Catalog of Selected Documents in Psychology.*

Books. The APA has published the following: *Psychology and the Problems of Society;* William James's *Unfinished Business; The Psychology Teacher's Resource Book: First Course; Rehabilitation Psychology; Research in Psychotherapy,* volumes I through III; *Pre-Conference Materials for Professional Preparation of Clinical Psychologists; The Psychology of Adult Development and Aging; 1973 APA Biographical Directory; Consolidated Roster for Psychology; 1974 Membership Register; Thesaurus of Psychological Index Terms.*

Proceedings. APA convention proceedings are: *1973 Complete Convention Proceedings; 1972 Complete Convention Proceedings; 1977 Complete Convention Proceedings.*

Miscellaneous. Other publications include: *Standards for Educational and Psychological Tests; Casebook on Ethical Standards of Psychologists (Updated); Publication Manual,* second edition; *Psychology: Where to Begin; Undergraduate Education in Psychology; Ethical Principles in the Conduct of Research with Human Participants; Graduate Study in Psychology 1975–1976; Keller's Personalized System of Instruction (PSI),* and other works.

Pamphlets. The APA has also published such pamphlets as "Careers in Psychology," "Psychology as a Profession," and "Ethical Standards of Psychologists."

A great many American universities, research centers, and other institutions have their own publishing houses, which print a great many scholarly books and journals in psychology. The bulk of scientific psychological work is published by the numerous private publishing houses.

Occupational Distribution

The occupational distribution of American psychologists is undergoing gradual yet distinct changes. Up to 1945 the majority of American psychologists were university teachers and/or researchers, but after World War II more and more psychologists turned to applied fields, especially industrial, clinical, and counseling psychology. In 1972, 41% of psychologists in the United States were college and university teachers and research workers and 39% were engaged in applied fields.

By 1978, 59% of American psychologists were engaged in clinical, counseling, community, and school psychology, and the other 41% percent were divided into general, experimental, research methods, comparative, social, developmental, physiological, personality, organizational-industrial, and other fields of psychology.

About 55% of the psychologists are employed by federal, state, and local governments; close to 35% work for nongovernmental institutions; and about 10% are self-employed. Close to 23% teach, about 17% engage in research, close to 18% work at a variety of administrative tasks, and over 40% provide services.

Opportunities for Foreign Psychologists

Some states accept foreign-trained psychologists while others rely on the foreign evaluation branch of the Department of Health, Education and Welfare of the federal government to assist them in evaluating training. The prospects for foreign-trained psychologists at this time are fair to good.

For information, one may consult American consulates and/or the American Psychological Association.

Table 1. American Psychological Association Membership 1974–1975

Division	Fellows	Members	Associates
General psychology	224	938	309
Teaching of psychology	273	1,716	489
Experimental psychology	411	743	
Evaluation and measurement	229	670	
Physiological and comparative psychology	125	504	
Developmental psychology	256	693	29
Personality and social psychology	392	3,347	905
Society for the psychological study of social issues	348	1,577	221
Psychology and the arts	46	257	60
Clinical psychology	746	3,198	
Consulting psychology	221	438	
Industrial and organizational psychology	235	846	164
Educational psychology	346	2,564	727
School psychology	126	1,404	917
Counseling psychology	220	1,784	277
Psychologists in public service	82	390	138
Military psychology	164	230	44
Adult development and aging	91	316	12
Society of engineering psychologists	96	270	41
Psychological aspects of disability	101	589	115
Consumer psychology	41	246	37
Philosophical psychology	89	319	38
Experimental analysis of behavior	87	1,196	189
History of psychology	97	324	29
Community psychology	112	874	96
Psychopharmacology	65	1,052	164
Psychotherapy	101	2,213	349
Psychological hypnosis	29	360	50
State psychological association affairs	125	1,033	32
Humanistic psychology	5	662	117
Mental retardation		473	
Population psychology		302	
Psychology of women		803	

Table 2. Doctoral Programs in Clinical, Counseling, and School Psychology in 1978 (Approved by the American Psychological Association)

Fully Approved Programs

CLINICAL PSYCHOLOGY

Adelphi University, Institute of Advanced Psychological Studies
Alabama, University of
American University
Arizona State University
Arizona, University of
Arkansas, University of
Boston University
Bowling Green State University
Brigham Young University
California, University of (Berkeley)
California, University of (Los Angeles)
Case Western Reserve University
Catholic University of America
Cincinnati, University of
City University of New York (City College)
Clark University
Colorado, University of
Connecticut, University of
Delaware, University of
Denver, University of
Duke University
Emory University
Florida State University
Florida, University of
Fordham University
Fuller Theological Seminary
George Washington University
Georgia State University
Georgia, University of
Hawaii, University of
Houston, University of

Illinois, University of
Illinois, University of, PsyD Program
Illinois, University of (Chicago Circle)
Indiana University
Iowa, University of
Kansas, University of
Kent State University
Kentucky, University of
Long Island University
Louisiana State University
Louisville, University of
Loyola University (Chicago)
Maine, University of
Manitoba, University of
Maryland, University of
Massachusetts, University of
McGill University
Memphis State University
Miami, University of (Florida)
Miami University (Ohio)
Michigan State University
Michigan, University of
Minnesota, University of
Mississippi, University of
Missouri, University of
Montana, University of
Nebraska, University of
Nevada, University of
New Mexico, University of
New York University
North Carolina, University of
North Dakota, University of
Northern Illinois University

Northwestern University Medical School, Department of Psychiatry and Behavioral Science
Ohio University
Oklahoma State University
Oregon, University of
Pennsylvania State University
Pennsylvania, University of
Pittsburgh, University of
Purdue University, Department of Psychological Sciences
Rhode Island, University of
Rochester, University of
Rutgers—The State University
St. Louis University
South Carolina, University of
South Dakota, University of
South Florida, University of
Southern California, University of
Southern Illinois University
State University of New York at Buffalo

State University of New York at Stony Brook
Syracuse University
Teachers College, Columbia University
Temple University
Tennessee, University of
Texas Tech University
Texas, University of
Utah, University of
Vanderbilt University
Vermont, University of
Virginia Commonwealth University
Washington State University
Washington, University of
Washington University (St. Louis)
Waterloo, University of
Wayne State University
West Virginia University
Wisconsin, University of
Wyoming, University of
Yale University

COUNSELING PSYCHOLOGY

Arizona State University, Department of Counselor Education
Catholic University of America
Colorado State University
Illinois, University of
Iowa State University
Kansas, University of, Interdepartmental Committee on Counseling Psychology
Maryland, University of
Michigan State University, Department of Counseling, Personnel Services, and Educational Psychology
Minnesota, University of, Department of Psychology
Minnesota, University of, Department of Counseling and Student Personnel Psychology, Psychoeducational Studies

Missouri, University of, Departments of Psychology, and Counseling and Personnel Services
Nebraska, University of, Department of Educational Psychology and Measurements
Notre Dame, University of
Ohio State University
Oregon, University of, Department of Counseling
Southern Illinois University
Teachers College, Columbia University
Temple University, Department of Counseling Psychology
Texas Tech University
Texas, University of, Department of Educational Psychology
Utah, University of, Department of Educational Psychology

Continued

Table 2. *(Continued)*

Fully Approved Programs

SCHOOL PSYCHOLOGY

Hofstra University, Department of
  School – Community Psychology
Minnesota, University of, Depart-
  ment of Psychoeducational
  Studies
Rhode Island, University of
Rutgers—The State University,

Graduate School of Applied and
  Professional Psychology, PsyD
  Program
South Carolina, University of
Teachers College, Columbia Uni-
  versity
Texas, University of, Department of
  Educational Psychology

Provisionally Approved Programs

Provisional approval is a candidacy category for emerging programs that are well along in their development or for programs that are strikingly innovative and therefore deviate from the criteria.

CLINICAL PSYCHOLOGY

DePaul University
Missouri, University of (St. Louis)
Rutgers—The State University,
  Graduate School of Applied and
  Professional Psychology, PsyD
  Program
Yeshiva University

COUNSELING PSYCHOLOGY

Florida, University of, Department
  of Psychology—Counselor Education

COMBINED PROFESSIONAL-SCIENTIFIC PSYCHOLOGY

Combined professional-scientific psychology is a new area of accreditation for programs that do not clearly fit the model for separate programs in clinical, counseling, and school psychology. This area of accreditation is defined as a combination of clinical, counseling, and/or school psychology.

George Peabody College for
  Teachers
Utah State University

Virginia, University of, Foundations
  of Education

Programs on Probation

CLINICAL PSYCHOLOGY
Ohio State University

COUNSELING PSYCHOLOGY
Michigan, University of

Table 3. Some Characteristics of Psychology Laws

State or province	Year of original approval	Coverage	Type of definition[a]	Education required[b]	Experience required (yrs)[b]	Examination mandatory[b]
Alabama (L)[c]	1963	Practice of psychology	S (P)	Doctoral	0	No
Alaska (L)	1967	Practice of psychology	S (P)	Doctoral	1	Yes
Alberta	1960	Psychologist	"0"	Master's	0	No
Arizona	1965	Psychologist	"0"	Doctoral	0	Yes[d]
Arkansas (L)	1955	Psychologist and psychological examiner		Doctoral	1	Yes
California (L)	1957	Psychologist	S (P)	Master's	0	Yes
Colorado (L)	1961	Psychology	S (P)	Doctoral	2[e]	No
Connecticut	1945	Psychologist	S	Doctoral	2 P	Yes
Delaware	1962	Psychologist	S	Doctoral	1 P	Yes
District of Columbia	1971	Practice of psychology	S (P)	Doctoral	1[f]	Yes
Florida (L)	1961	Practice of psychology	S (P)	Doctoral	2	Yes
Georgia (L)	1951	Practice of applied psychology	S	Doctoral	2[e]	Yes
Hawaii (L)	1967	Practice of psychology	S	Doctoral	1	No
Idaho (L)	1963	Practice of psychology	S (P)	Doctoral	0	Yes
Illinois	1963	Psychologist	S (P)	Doctoral	2 P	No
Indiana	1969	Psychologist in private practice	S	Doctoral	2	Yes
		Psychologist, basic	S	Doctoral	3 P	Yes
Iowa	1974	Practice of psychology	S	Doctoral	0	Yes
				Doctoral	1 P	Yes
		Practice of psychology associate		Master's	5	Yes
				Master's	0	Yes

Continued

Table 3. (Continued)

State or province	Year of original approval	Coverage	Type of definition[a]	Education required[b]	Experience required (yrs)[b]	Examination mandatory[b]
Kansas	1967	Psychologist	S	Doctoral	2	Yes[d]
Kentucky (L)	1948	Practice of psychology	S	Doctoral	1	Yes
Louisiana	1964	Psychologist	S (P)	Doctoral	2 P	Yes
Maine (L)	1953	Psychologist	S (P)	Doctoral	2	Yes
		Psychological examiner		Master's 1	Yes	
Manitoba	1966	Psychologist	None	Doctoral	0	Yes
Maryland	1957	Psychologist	S	Doctoral	2[e]	Yes
Massachusetts (L)	1971	Practice of psychology	S (P)	Doctoral	2[e]	Yes
Michigan	1959	Consulting psychologist	S	Doctoral	5	Yes
		Psychologist		Doctoral	1	No
		Psychological examiner or technician		Master's	1	No
Minnesota (L)	1951	Consulting psychologist	S	Doctoral	2 P	Yes
		Psychologist		Masters	2 P	Yes
Mississippi	1966	Psychologist	S	Doctoral	1	No
Montana (L)	1971	Practice of psychology	S (P)	Doctoral	2 P	Yes
Nebraska (L)	1967	Practice of psychology	S (P)	Doctoral	0	Yes
Nevada	1963	Psychologist	"0"	Doctoral	1 P	Yes
New Brunswick	1967	Psychologist	"0"	Doctoral	1	Yes
New Hampshire	1957	Psychologist		Doctoral	2	Yes

State/Province	Year	Title	Type	Degree	Number	Reciprocity
New Jersey (L)	1966	Practice of psychology	S (P)	Doctoral	2^e	Yes
New Mexico	1963	Psychologist	S	Doctoral	2 P	Yes
New York	1956	Psychologist	S (P)^g	Doctoral	2	Yes
North Carolina (L)	1967	Psychologist	S (P)	Doctoral	2 P	Yes
		Psychological examiner		Master's	0	Yes
North Dakota	1967	Psychologist	S	Doctoral	0	Yes
Ohio (L)	1972	Practice of psychology	S (P)	Doctoral	2^e	Yes
		Practice of school psychology	S	Master's	1	Yes
Oklahoma (L)	1965	Practice of psychology	S	Doctoral	2	Yes
Ontario	1960	Psychologist	"O"	Doctoral	1	Yes
Oregon (L)	1973	Practice of psychology	S (P)	Doctoral	2	Yes
		Psychologist's associate		Master's	3	Yes
Pennsylvania (L)	1972	Practice of psychology	S	Doctoral	2 P	Yes
				Master's	4 P	Yes
Quebec	1962	Psychologist	S	Doctoral or Masters	0	No
Rhode Island	1969	Psychologist	S	Doctoral	0	No
Saskatchewan	1962	Reg. psychologist	"O"	Doctoral	2^e	Yes
South Carolina (L)	1968	Practice of psychology	S (P)	Doctoral	0	No
Tennessee (L)	1953	Psychologist	S (P)	Doctoral	1^h	No
		Psychological examiner		Master's	0	Yes
Texas (L)	1969	Psychologist	"O"	Doctoral	2^e	Yes
Utah	1959	Psychologist	S	Doctoral	2	Yes
Virginia (L)	1946	Practice of psychology	S (P)	Doctoral	2 P^i	Yes

Continued

Table 3. (Continued)

State or province	Year of original approval	Coverage	Type of definition[a]	Education required[b]	Experience required (yrs)[b]	Examination mandatory[b]
Washington	1955	Psychologist	S (P)	Doctoral	1 P	Yes
West Virginia (L)	1970	Practice of psychology	S (P)	Doctoral	2 P	Yes
				Master's	8 P	Yes
Wisconsin (L)	1969	Practice of psychology	S (P)	Doctoral	1	No
Wyoming	1965	Psychologist	S (P)	Doctoral	0	Yes

[a] S means a specific definition; (P) means that psychotherapy is included; "0" means a circular definition—a person is a psychologist when he calls himself one and does psychological work.

[b] These three columns all refer to postgraduate provisions; they do not reflect the requirements under reciprocal endorsement provisions. P means postdoctoral (or post-master's in the case of West Virginia, Minnesota, and Pennsylvania). In connection with the examination, "No" is shown if the examining board has any authority in the law to waive it.

[c] (L) means licensing law, penalizing the practice of psychology by any title without a license.

[d] The examination under the Arizona law is unassembled, consisting of an evaluation of credentials submitted by the applicant. In Kansas, the examination may be either assembled or unassembled.

[e] One of the 2 years must be postdoctoral.

[f] Two years of experience are required if the field is clinical psychology.

[g] The definition in New York's law is circular; there is a specific definition, including psychotherapy, in the regulations (of the commissioner of education).

[h] The 1 year of experience is required if the field is clinical psychology; there is no experience requirement otherwise.

[i] Clinical psychologists must have completed an internship or practicum of at least 1 year.

Table 4. Some Characteristics of Non-statutory Psychology Provisions[a, b]

State or province	Year adopted	Coverage	Education required[c]	Experience required (yrs.)[c]	Examination Mandatory[c]	Reciprocity[d]
British Columbia	1964	Certified psychologist	Doctoral	2	Yes	Yes (A)
Missouri	1958	Psychologist	Doctoral	1	No	Yes
South Dakota	1961	Psychological specialist[e]	Doctoral	2	No	Yes
		Psychologist	Master's	5	No	Yes
Vermont	1966	Certified psychologist	Doctoral	1	Yes	Yes
			Master's	3	Yes	Yes

[a]Prepared by the Professional Affairs Office, American Psychological Association, October 1974.
[b]Nonstatutory certification programs are administered by the state or provincial psychological association.
[c]These three columns all are in terms of postgraduate provisions; they do not reflect requirements under reciprocal endorsement provisions.
[d]"Reciprocity" means endorsement of another state's certificate or license, if standards are not lower, to waive the examination. (A) means that the examination may be waived for holders of the diploma from the American Board of Professional Psychology.
[e]Specialties are clinical, counseling, or industrial psychology.

Uruguay[1]

National Organization

The national psychological organization in Uruguay is the
Sociedad de Psicología del Uruguay
Uruguayan Society of Psychology
25 de Mayo 535, Esc. 9
Montevideo, Uruguay
The official language is Spanish.

Internal Structure

The sociedad was organized in December 1953 and is
ruled by the comisión directiva (executive committee), which
consists of president, vice-president, secretary, recording secretary, treasurer, and four members. The tasks of the comisión
directiva are to promote psychology as a science and as a
profession, to plan scientific projects and implement them, to
form divisions and committees, etc. The comisión directiva is
checked by the members.

Membership

There are 429 members in the sociedad divided into the
following categories: titulares, adherentes, de honor, and cor-
respondientes. The 72 titulares have to spend at least 1 year as

[1]Based on information supplied by Julietta Lagomarsino, secretary, Sociedad
de Psicología del Uruguay, and other sources.

regular (adherentes) members. The 322 regular members have been admitted to the sociedad on the basis of a university degree. The two honorary members have made an outstanding contribution to psychology.

Major Activities

The main activities of the sociedad are publication of a journal, and organization of conferences and postgraduate courses and seminars.

Education and Training

The school of psychology, Escuela Universitaria de Psicología of the Universidad de la República in Montevideo, offers a many-sided program in psychology that includes neurophysiology, experimental psychology, statistics, research design, philosophy of science, and comparative, developmental, social, and applied psychology. It grants the titles of psicólo, psicólogo especializado, and on the highest level, doctor en psicología.

Research

The Psychological Institute of the Universidad de la República engages in research in such diversified fields as projective techniques, mental measurements, and developmental psychology.

Occupational Distribution

Psychologists in Uruguay are employed by the university, Teachers College (Instituto Normal), and the educational systems. Clinical psychologists work mostly as diplomaticians and child therapists.

Opportunities for Foreign Psychologists

Foreign psychologists interested in visiting or permanent positions in Uruguay should contact either the Sociedad de Psicología del Uruguay at the above address or the

Universidad de la República
Escuela de Psicología
Avenida 18 de Julio 1824
Montevideo, Uruguay

Venezuela[1]

National Organization

The national psychological organization of Venezuela is the
Colegio de Psicólogos de Venezuela
Apartado 62558 Chacao
Caracas 106, Venezuela
The official language is Spanish.

Internal Structure

The colegio is governed by (1) the executive committee
(junta directiva), which is composed of seven members: president, vice-president, general secretary, treasurer, and three
members; (2) the disciplinary tribunal (tribunal disciplinario nacional), which has three principal members and three substitute
members; (3) special sections in some geographical areas of the
country, each section having an executive committee similar to
the central one. These sections (seccionales) function in coordination with the central body.

The responsibilities of the executive committee are (1) representation of the national organization; (2) enforcement of the
resolutions of the general assembly of all members; (3) designation of ad hoc commissions in order to fulfill the objectives of
the organization (matters such as trade unions, social services,
credentials, public relations, relations with other professional
organizations, publications).

[1]Based on information supplied by Erik Becker, president, Colegio de
Psicólogos de Venezuela, and other sources.

The function of the disciplinary tribunal is vigilance in the fulfillment of the ethical code.

The sections' executive committees are responsible in a manner similar to that of the central body in regard to their particular region.

The members of all these offices are elected for a year and they may be reelected for a second period. The voters are all the active members.

Membership

The total number of members is 1,323 (compared with the total number of psychologists in Venezuela, which is 2,000).

Categories of membership, with their approximate number, are as follows: active—1,253, provisional—54, honorary —1, student (as of 1977)—15.

The colegio has seven divisions, with their approximate number as follows: clinical psychology—50, counseling psychology—20, dynamic psychology—15, humanistic psychology—20, industrial psychology—20, school psychology—25, social psychology—30.

Membership Requirements

For active members, the degree of licenciado en psicología offered by a national university is necessary. Provisional members should hold a degree equivalent to the one offered by the national universities, properly certified by the country's consulate, and with evidence of revalidation process of the degree at any of the national universities. Honorary members are nonpsychologists, with merits at a scientific or professional level.

Major Activities

Every 3 months a national assembly is held that is open to all active members. These assemblies deal with legal issues to be presented to the Parliament of Venezuela, reorganization of the national organization, social services (medical care, life insurance, etc.) for psychologists, and achievement of all other tasks of the colegio. In addition, the colegio organizes a celebration of Psychologists' Day and a forum concerning the fields of applied psychology in Venezuela as well as a Latin American seminar on social psychology, held at Caracas and organized by the Society of Social Psychology. It also prepares the *Jornadas Nacionales de Psicología*.

Education and Training

There are two schools currently offering training in psychology. They are the Universidad Central de Venezuela, Facultad de Humanidades y Educación, Escuela de Psicología, Ciudad Universitaria, Caracas (a governmental institution with free tuition); and Universidad Católica Andres Bello, Escuela de Psicología, Facultad de Humanidades, La Vega-Montalbán, Caracas. Two universities offer graduate courses on a master's level: the Universidad Central de Venezuela and the Universidad Simón Bolívar.

Universidad Central de Venezuela (UCV). From 1960 to 1971 it offered a degree of licenciado en psicología. Since 1972 it has offered a degree of licenciado en psicología "with mention in clinical psychology, school psychology, counseling psychology, industrial psychology, social psychology," or "without mention" (which are special curricula at the same level).

Since 1975 they have offered courses for the master's degree.

Universidad Católica Andres Bello (UCAB). This university offers a degree of licenciado en psicología. The average number of students in each program is as follows: clinical psychology—15, school—18, counseling—10, industrial—25, social—10, "without mention"—2. The average number of students licensed each year is 65.

Both universities function under the National Council of

Universities (Consejo Nacional de Universidades), a governmental organ that supervises the curricula and other requirements for the accreditation of the degrees.

The national psychological organization, the colegio, has a delegate (active member) to the specific academic council of each school of psychology at each university, and through these members it makes suggestions concerning the academic organization of psychological training in the country.

The students at the UCV should cover a number of credits in a minimum of 10 terms (5 years) of university training and must present a thesis before obtaining the degree of licenciado en psicología (6 terms in general training and 4 terms of specialization). The credits are obtained through examinations at the end of each term.

After 5 years of training and approval of the examinations, the student at UCAB must present a thesis before obtaining the degree. The postgraduate courses require a special number of credits and a thesis for the master's degree.

Legal Status

As the legal instrument for psychologists (ley de ejercicio de la psicología) has not been approved yet by the parliament, there is no compulsory requirement of registration at the national organization before working in the field. The only requirement is the degree offered by the national universities.

The colegio has an ethics code, but it has no legal compulsory status. The psychologist who has violated these internal rules is subject to the study of the disciplinary tribunal.

Research

There is no government agency specifically doing research in psychology, but several ministries have "research departments" that do research in psychological areas (i.e., Ministry of Education, Ministry of Justice, Ministry of Health and Social Security). There are some official research institutes, such as

CONICIT (Consejo Nacional de Investigaciones Científicas y Tecnologícas) and IVIC (Instituto Venezolano de Investigaciones Científicas), that also do some research in this area. All these institutions are financed by the government.

The Universidad Central de Venezuela (Facultad de Humanidades y Educación, Instituto de Psicología) has a special research institute in psychology. It is financed by the university and there is also the possibility of obtaining grants for specific research from other sources. The university also has a research and specialization center (CENDES), which works on nonspecialized psychological issues.

There is some research work done at different schools in several faculties of the university, and there are some private research centers working in the areas of social and industrial psychology.

Publications

Journals. The national psychological organization recently started a quarterly journal. In addition, the School of Psychology of the Universidad Central de Venezuela also started a quarterly journal, *Psicología,* in 1974. The address of the journal is Escuela de Psicología, Universidad Central de Venezuela, Ciudad Universitaria, Caracas. Volume 1, number 1 through volume 2 number 1 appeared by March 1975, and volume 2 number 2 through number 4 appeared by December 1975.

Books. It is very difficult to estimate the number of books published per year. Some recent books are mentioned below:

Dembo, Miriam and Penfold, Julia, *Condicionamiento Instrumental de Requestas Autonómas.*

Ruiz, Robert, *El papel de la Teoría en la Behaviorismo.* [B. F. Skinner.]

Tavella, Nicolas, *Los Instrumentos Psicométricos en la Dianostico del Retardado Mental.*

Tavella, Nicolas, *El Análisis de los Items en la Construcción de Instrumentos Psicométricos.*

Tavella, Nicolas, *Análisis de Items: Ejercicios.*
All these books have been edited by the School of
Psychology, UCV.

Occupational Distribution

In approximate numbers, the psychologists in Venezuela
work in the following positions: university positions—300,
teachers in secondary education—100, school psychologists—150, vocational counselors—120, rehabilitation
counselors—30; clinical psychologists in hospitals—20, clinical psychologists in private practice—100, research—80, industrial psychologists—200, family counselors—50, dynamic
groups—60.

Opportunities for Foreign Psychologists

Foreign-trained psychologists up until now have been able
to work in the country with only their degree certificates (properly backed by their consulate), but they should apply for revalidation procedures at any of the national universities mentioned above. At the national organization they have been accepted as "provisional members." Inquiries should be addressed to the national organization.

Yugoslavia[1] (Socialist Federal Republic of Yugoslavia, SFRJ)

National Organization

The national psychological organization in Yugoslavia is:

Yugoslovenski Udruzenje Psihologa
c/o Dr. A. Dolinar
Odenje za Psihologiju
Filozofsky Fakultet
61000 Ljubljana
Yugoslavia

The address of the central office changes from year to year.

The official languages are Serbo-Croatian, Slovene, and Macedonian.

Internal Structure

The Yugoslav Psychological Association consists of the six psychological associations, one in each republic, as Yugoslavia has six republics. The executive committee moves every year

---

[1]Based on information supplied by various sources.

from one republic to another. Administrative work is done in the office of the psychological association of the republic that is th residence of that year's president.

The electoral system of the executive council is determined by the rules of the Yugoslav Psychological Association. The psychological association of each of the six republics has one delegate.

Membership

A member of the psychological association of any republic of SFRJ is a member of the Yugoslav Psychological Association as well. The total number is 1,350. All members are psychologists with university degrees.

The psychological associations of every republic organize working sections, such as, sections for clinical psychology or sections for school psychology.

Membership Requirements

The psychological associations of each republic define their own terms of membership.

Major Activities

The major activities of the association are publishing of reviews, organizing a congress of psychologists for all of Yugoslavia every 3 years, representing the psychological associations of the republics at the International Union of Psychological Science.

Education and Training

All six Yugoslav universities offer courses in psychology; four of them offer diplomas in psychology and, at a more advanced level, a master's degree and a doctorate. The Belgrade University offers advanced training in clinical, educational, and industrial psychology. The universities in Skoplje, Zagreb, and Ljubljana are similar. All Yugoslav universities offer courses in experimental development, social, personality, motivation, and other fields in psychology.

The highest degree in psychology is doctor of psychological science.

Legal Status

This is not settled for all fields where psychologists are working. It is different in various republics of Yugoslavia; however, school and clinical psychologists are legally recognized.

Research and Publications

The universities of Belgrade, Zagreb, Ljubljana, and Nis Skoplje conduct research in developmental, social, and educational psychology.

The Zavod Za Produktivnost, SRS Ljubljana Parmova 33 and Zavod SRS Za Varstvo Pri Delu, Ljubljana Bohoriceva 22a conduct research in industrial psychology.

A journal, *Revija za psihologiju,* is published in Zagreb.

Occupational Distribution

All Yugoslav psychologists are employed by the federal government or by the governments of the six republics.

Opportunities for Foreign Psychologists

Inquiries should be directed to the Yugoslav consulates.